How to Have a
YOGA BODY

CLAUDIA AZULA

ISBN: 9798764480565

CONTENTS

INTRODUCTION

I first felt a call to dedicate myself to yoga during an introductory class twenty-five years ago. At the end of that class, the teacher instructed us to relax in a modification of the corpse pose in which we laid on the floor, facing up, with our knees opened to the side. I arranged my body carefully and lay there for a while, as instructed, savoring the silence. As I melted into relaxation, my hips felt an opening and a release. After a few more minutes, something unexpected happened: tears began flowing down my face. Back then, relaxing my hips was a new sensation. As it happened, some old, painful memories came over me, and I started crying. I became embarrassed and uncomfortable because I didn't want to show vulnerability, and I feared being ridiculed. The teacher saw me, gave me a moment, and addressed everyone in the class by saying, "releasing emotions is not unusual in this pose because trauma is stored in the hips." I immediately felt comforted by her words and the shame went away. Before that day, I never thought I could release *feelings* through my body, and it piqued my curiosity. This new information hooked me. I wanted to learn more about these techniques that could go further than exercise and affect deeper aspects of my life.

Throughout years of practice, I have learned many yoga techniques, born thousands of years ago, which are helping me to be healthy and navigate the strong emotions within my body. Yoga has given me a new way of looking at myself and the world around me. My practice has taken me from a perception of my body as a crude physical instrument to a more subtle understanding of its connection to my emotions, breath, wisdom, and spirit.

One of the most interesting lessons that I've learned through my practice is that I don't need to change much of my approach to life, but simply remove obstacles that make me inflexible in both body and mind. This change in perception and attitude toward life is about identifying and releasing blockages. It's very much like Michelangelo approaching a piece of marble and, in his mind, already seeing the beautiful sculpture hidden within it. All he has to do to reveal his vision is chip away what doesn't belong.

I could describe the role you are about to undertake with a word I invented, "innernaut." Instead of exploring the universe of outer space, as an astronaut would, you will explore the fascinating subtleties of your own inner universe.

The practices in this book are based on two major works of yoga. One is *The Yoga Sutras of Patanjali*. The sutras are composed of 196 lines of cryptic text that focus mostly on intellectual comprehension with some practical ways of digging deep. In the other textbook, *The Hatha Yoga Pradipika*, the yogi Swatamarama elaborates on postures and breathing techniques. For example, where Patanjali describes asanas with only one line, "asana must be steady and comfortable," the *Hatha Yoga Pradipika* describes specific techniques and lists dozens of poses. But the end goal of yoga is always the same: to arrive at enlightenment or complete freedom from preconceived lines of thought and actions. The *Yoga Sutras* defines yoga in its first line, "yoga is the cessation of the fluctuations of the mind." We arrive at yoga when we can completely let go of all negative and unnecessary thinking. *The Hatha Yoga Pradipika* goes one step forward because it recognizes that stopping all negative thinking is not easy, and so it describes cleansings for the body, breath, and actions.

My goal is to help you achieve a flexible and strong body and access your innate wisdom and spiritual connection. My intention is to help you remove all obstacles to your spirit. I will offer you techniques that you can learn and keep, regardless of where you are or what your conditions may be. The practices in this book will produce tangible and noticeable results in your body, and if you dedicate yourself to them in a balanced way, they will also provide a grounded approach to the art of living a spiritual life.

An important thing to remember is that your body is perfect exactly the way it is. Nobody has an inadequate body. What yoga can do is chip away at obstacles such as bad posture, labored breathing and emotional blocks that prevent your body from reaching its full potential.

What to Expect

The first chapter of this book focuses on the physical body. While practicing on the mat, you may become aware of muscles you have never felt before and learn about new ones. Changes will happen naturally and over time. Your body will shine and become supple and beautiful in its own way and at its own pace. Cleansing techniques will help your body perform optimally.

The second chapter addresses the most underappreciated function of the body: breathing. You will learn proper breathing techniques and learn how improper breathing can disrupt your ability to function both physically and emotionally.

The third chapter explores the emotional yoga body. You will learn how emotional baggage and past traumas can negatively affect physical and spiritual health and prevent you from advancing in your practice. You will learn exercises to release anger and fear.

The fourth chapter accesses the power of discrimination and wisdom. You will learn how to differentiate truth from illusion, and face life on its own terms. In plain words, this is the subtle level where insanity ends, and your heart overflows with love. At this stage, you will use a newfound self-love and compassion to forgive yourself and others.

The fifth chapter explores the joyous results of a daily practice. You will begin to strengthen what I call your spiritual muscle. At this stage you can expect to live with contentment and to experience synchronicities that can only come from a place of depth and spirit.

Yoga uses the metaphor of chakras, or centers of energy, that allow the energy of enlightenment to flow from the bottom of the spine to the top of the head. As we travel through each subtle body, I will identify the chakras we are working on opening. The optimal function of these centers of energy leads to a fulfilling life.

THERE ARE SEVEN CHAKRAS:

First chakra: Root, or Muladhara
Located at the base of the spine, the root chakra affects your physical body and all life experiences and situations.

Second chakra: Svadhisthana
Located one inch below the belly button, this chakra allows the flourishing of your creativity. It also influences the ability to bring forth new life.

Third chakra: Manipura
Lying in the navel, it is responsible for helping process information,

exerting your will, and offering new ideas to the world.

Fourth chakra: Anahata
Located at the heart, this chakra rules unconditional love, self-esteem, and compassion.

Fifth chakra: Vishuddha
Located in the throat, this chakra is the one that gives our true voice and talents expression.

Sixth chakra: Ajna
Located in the third eye, this chakra is the seat of consciousness. It is the spiritual center, and it opens intuition, imagination, insightfulness, and other qualities whose sources are in the divinity of Spirit.

Seventh chakra: Sahasrara
Located at the crown of the head, it symbolizes enlightenment, the ability to be completely present without distraction from preconceived beliefs.

Companion Videos

The ten videos that accompany this book target specific areas of the body and breath. The last video, number ten, is a comprehensive class that contains the most powerful postures of each of the previous classes. You can follow the videos in order, or you can use the one you need for a specific reason on a certain day. The last video is a complete practice with postures to address all your subtle bodies. Learn this last class by heart and you will have a comprehensive go-to class within your mind to practice anytime and anywhere you go.

The companion videos can be found in a playlist on my YouTube channel: www.YouTube.com/c/ClaudiaAzula

What You Will Need

- A yoga mat
- A notebook
- A yoga block (this is optional but helpful for yoga beginners. Blocks are useful in accommodating your body to new postures.)
- A comfortable yoga blanket that will help you relax

I have curated some quality options for these tools that won't break the bank. These recommendations can be found in the resources page at the end of the book.

CHAPTER 1

The Physical YOGA BODY

I'll admit, I became passionate about yoga because I wanted to experience the inner glow that yogis exude, and to look good naked! I wanted to improve my body, and I wanted to feel better. With this motivation, I jumped into the world of yoga by enrolling in classes that involved a daily commitment. On my first day, I went to class in the wrong clothes. I had too many layers of t-shirts and leg warmers and my body overheated. I didn't expect to sweat so much. When I looked at myself in the mirror afterward, I could see that despite my exhaustion, my body was shining and there was a sparkle in my eyes. From that day on, my body changed, slowly. My muscles became stronger and more flexible and my range of movement improved. Within a year, I lost thirty pounds. Today, I am grateful for how wonderful I feel. I don't think that pursuing a better body is a shallow motivation for starting yoga and don't let anyone tell you otherwise. I think that wanting a strong and beautiful physical body is an intelligent choice.

When we think of yoga, we picture bodies moving through space in graceful and elegant poses. When we watch others practice, we join them by visualizing how the movements would feel in our bodies. We tell ourselves, "Oh, that must feel goooood," or maybe, "I could never do that and hope I never have to." Just by watching, we begin to experience the sensations of yoga, and something profound awakens.

Shortly after committing to daily asana practice at the studio, I started comparing my experience with others in the class. I was often in awe of how they moved. They were standing on their hands without using a wall for balance, dropping backward from a standing position onto the floor, and doing extreme splits and other dramatic contortions. I started friendships with most of these women. Sometimes we talked about our jobs and laughed about the hardships of dating in New York or issues with family. Other times we shared how we felt after that day's practice. A friend said, "I feel pain moving around my body every single day. One day it's in my shoulder and the next in my hips, but it's the good kind of pain." Another said, "I don't know why the teacher doesn't help me with the poses. I need more attention or I will never get it." I was fascinated by how they had been practicing longer than me and how they experienced their bodies. I was also a bit intimidated by the names of all the asanas and how many there were. I thought I would never learn them all. Some of the poses had names that represented animals, like cobra or jumping crocodile. Others had plain names, like one leg stretch. It was overwhelming for me to see how much there was to learn. But the daily and consistent ritual of getting on the mat taught me that there was no need to master it all at once. Asanas don't come quickly because the body needs to re-invent itself to enter them. Students often ask how long it might take to touch the floor in a forward bend. Although there is no universal answer, I find that with daily practice, they may move forward by an inch per month. This is just a reference based on my experience, but it gives a general idea.

As you learn new asanas, be patient with your body. As you experience new sensations, try to endure the discomfort and breathe. When you relax into a pose you will find your edge, which is the line between what you can do and the version of the asana you see a teacher do.

With time, you will ease into the pose, slowly moving into new levels of flexibility and strength. You will discover new creases in your skin, you will feel parts of your body you may not have felt in years, and perhaps get into positions that will make you blush. Every pose will bring a level of bewilderment. As you awaken muscles, ligaments, tissues, joints, etc., you will begin to move elegantly, feel better, and in some cases, lose weight. Patience and calm breathing are the necessary ingredients to refine your body from unpolished to malleable.

Remember that if it hurts, it's not yoga. When entering asanas, look for the sweet spot before you feel any strain but you are also not entirely comfortable. Once there, breathe. The more you stay in a pose with elongated inhales and exhales, the more you will feel your body respond. Instead of breathing deeply, which is exhausting, think about making the length of inhalation and exhalation smooth, long, and even. In this way, after a few slow breaths in any pose, you will feel a release. The body will give in and adapt.

Yoga Restores Your Body to Health

Yoga is a type of tricky medicine. Sometimes when I learn new poses, I feel awkward and resent the posture, but I have learned that the discomfort of a new asana works like a preventive type of health insurance. Tender new sensations today mean better health in the future. For example, I may be uneasy as I practice a deep twist, but my digestive system will become better prepared to release toxins and process nutrients. Bodies are resilient, and they learn quickly. Asanas guide them to do their work more efficiently.

The first YouTube video companion to this book offers a practice you can start immediately. It demonstrates two essential sequences, the sun salutations. Think of these two fluid routines as the bread and butter of your physical practice. I recommend repeating them until you know them by heart. Choose a time of day to practice that works best for you. In the morning, your body will be tighter, but your mind will be clear. In the afternoon, your body will be more pliable, but your mind will be active. Make your practice personal. Rolling out the mat and practicing every day may be challenging in the beginning because developing a new discipline can be difficult. I encourage you to be gentle with yourself and try to build a ritual at first. If you find that you cannot practice one day, just unroll the mat, stand at the edge of it, take one breath and end your practice there. That's it. You can roll the mat back and continue with your day. What this does is help you build a routine. If you incorporate this small detail into your day, maybe one morning you might decide to do a little more than take one breath, and who knows? You may end up watching one of the videos and practicing for twenty minutes or more. Investigate and learn from your body, what time does it prefer to practice? Which of the classes does it like best? Does it want a short routine with specific postures, or would it rather go to the comprehensive set of asanas of the tenth video? When you start, don't judge, let your body play with the practice and do what you can. Train your body with love and care and explore it as if you were an archeologist discovering a new site. Leave no detail unexamined.

LET GO

Drawing by Nathalie Jaspar

The Story of the Sun Salutations

The practice of sun salutations originated a century ago when a renowned teacher combined elements of yoga and bodybuilding. This teacher, TK Krishnamacharya, was a yogi that gained fame during the 1920s for his extreme yoga demonstrations. His performances would typically begin with difficult asanas and progress to amazing feats such as lifting heavy objects with his teeth or actually stopping his heart. His traveling shows and demonstrations are partially responsible for the widespread popularity of yoga today.

In the early 1930s, after years of practicing yoga, Krishnamacharya caught the attention of the Maharaja of Mysore, who was interested in spiritual and physical practices. To help promote health initiatives, The Maharaja asked Krishnamacharya to open a yoga school and offered him a wing of his palace to teach. But the Maharaja was not only interested in yoga, he also promoted other types of exercise. In another wing of his palace, military teachers imparted vigorous physical training to young soldiers. It was there that Krishnamacharya got his inspiration to blend the breathing and flowing poetry of yoga with the regimented and strong discipline of warriors. The sun salutations he created became the most exciting mix of ancient and modern techniques of yoga. Today, most teachers start their asana classes with them. The beauty of the salutations is that they are self-contained practices. They incorporate strong standing poses, push-ups, forward and backbends, and a conscious way of breathing.

Don't wait. I encourage you to start the first video companion class right away. This book is meant to be more than a reading exercise. It promotes an immersive experience. If you start practicing, the words in the book will resonate with you when you are on the mat, and they will provide a comprehensive way to make the practice your own.

The Practice

- Before you take the class for the sun salutations, grab your notebook, and write a few words that describe how you are feeling.
- If you have never practiced the salutations before, you may want to watch the video before you get on the mat.
- Practice with the video.
- After practice, write a few words that now describe your feelings.
- Note how your body is feeling. Document any tension or places where you feel discomfort.
- Continue this practice every day and keep writing what you discover.

Yoga Has No Levels

Levels like "advanced" or "master" are artificial and unnecessary. They can lead you to think you are less than, or better than, others. Instead of comparing yourself to others, use your energy to move deeper into the subtleties of your own experience. Your yoga practice is personal. The only "levels" of yoga that are important are your level of enjoyment and your sense of progress.

Yoga is about self-love and self-respect. It is about evolving by becoming less rigid. When I teach, I know that enforcing strict authority and discipline to a class of students who feel tired, stressed, and frustrated won't work. If we are tense, the body will rebel. That is why so many forceful exercise challenges are left behind within a few days.

Yoga is a mechanism for finding compassion for ourselves. Approach the practice searching for intimacy instead of intensity. You will grow in closeness with your body as you get to know it, and there is nothing a body likes more than having attention payed to it. And remember to keep it light. Developing a sense of humor goes hand in hand with yoga. Your body is playful regardless of your age. Have fun with it.

Yoga Feels Beautiful

In one simple and elegant line from *The Yoga Sutras*, Patanjali says that yoga asanas must be steady and comfortable. That's it. He says nothing else about them. Other ancient texts describe asanas as gestures, or mudras, which embody special energies. Finding the form of an asana within your body unlocks the internal power it offers. As you find steadiness and comfort in a pose, the figure you create becomes a mudra, or a seal of energy, that contains innate wisdom.

A daily practice of yoga asanas is an invitation to engage in a form of body poetry, a flow from one form to another and an exploration of how your body responds. When you enter poses with steadiness and comfort, you access the symbolic power of your body. When you watch an experienced yogi, you can appreciate their refinement as they arrive at the final form of a posture. When you practice with the videos, do what you can but visualize the final gesture of a pose. It doesn't matter how far you can go on a particular day, but the practice gets more interesting if you can visualize the final form and work toward embodying it. Doing this will help you stay alert to each detail.

All postures in yoga play with the tension of opposites. If you are positioned in a forward bend, there are many forces and counterforces at work. For example, in a triangle pose, which we explore in depth on the second YouTube video class, the lower part of your spine aims to square the hips down toward the mat, while the thoracic and cervical spine open and twist upward, looking at the sky. There is a slight tension between the lower part of the body facing down and the upper part facing up which produces a twist. The triangle pose may look like a standing posture that will strengthen the legs, but it is much more than that as you will see when you start feeling the twist. Visualizing the final form of a posture will consciously and unconsciously inform your body of the subtle movements it needs to approximate the seal of energy that the full pose will bring.

One of my favorite postures is downward facing dog. There are so many things happening at once that it has taken me years to digest how rich it is. At first sight, it may look like you are just making a triangle with the floor and your body, but if you pay attention to the fine details, you will feel a delightful stretching of the whole back of your body. When you are in the pose, imagine that your skin is stretching from the back of your heels, through the back of your legs all the way to the top of the tailbone and then down through your spine and to the top of your head. Feel the skin. For a deeper effect, tighten your quadriceps as if you wanted them to grab the femur bones, which are the big bones of your upper legs. This will help you pull your stomach in and deepen the stretch of your back. Every pose has within it a universe of sensations. No matter how long I practice, there is always a nuance to discover, a new sensation, and a new challenge. If you wake up to each pose and start taking delight in each tiny movement, instead of just going through the motions, the seal of energy will find you. When it does, the experience will be unique and yours alone. The body will begin revealing its magnificent power and brightness. You will begin to understand the phrase: "your body is a temple." There is a mystical quality to the exploration of the physical body, and yoga has made an art out of it.

The Ground Rules

As in most spiritual traditions, yoga sets ground rules from the beginning by establishing a moral compass. There are observances and restraints, dos and don'ts. Most spiritual traditions have their own laws or suggestions for daily living. Within the physical body chapter, I wanted to bring attention to how these conducts apply to the body as well.

Yoga Sutra 2.30 lists non-harming, truthfulness, non-stealing, sexual restraint, and non-greed as the restraints. These restraints are called yamas, and they apply to the body.

For example, non-harming asks us to refrain from any type of yoga that pushes us into a pose or a practice that we are not ready for. If you allow yourself or others to push you to the point of physical pain, anxiety and stress will follow. You may still learn a lesson because pain is a teacher, but you will not reap the healing benefits that slow and steady progress bring. When we push, we disregard truthfulness. We justify greed, letting it pass for effort. But when it comes to our bodies, greed is dangerous.

Truthfulness is not always clearly defined. For example, if you are in a business meeting and need a bathroom break, you may want to hold on because you feel the timing is not convenient. This is a disregard for the body, and although it will cooperate, the negative effects will add up unless you address the psychological fear that prevents you from attending to its needs. We steal from ourselves when we over-extend or deny what our bodies need. We ignore self-care in the name of working hard, looking strong, and so on. These are tendencies of the mind that end up affecting the body. The mind may say, "If you leave this meeting now, the managers won't like you," or "you will look weak if you take a break." When the mind gets in the way of self-care, there is a deeper problem, which we will address as we go further. But for the time being, the moment you feel pain or a call of nature, see it as a request from your body and listen. Then thank it for communicating with you and respect its wishes.

When it comes to sex, practicing yoga means that we enjoy our sexuality thoughtfully. It's not good to shy away from it by falling into sexual and social anorexia, but it's also not good to act out by seeking sex, intrigue, or the thrill of sexual encounters in order to avoid facing our feelings. We need to strive to find a happy medium that brings us the intimacy we desire without causing harm to ourselves or others.

Sexual restraint, as suggested by the *Yoga Sutras*, means that we enjoy sex while being conscious of possible consequences. It's great to seek a loving intimacy with a partner, but this can only happen when we can first be intimate with ourselves. We should be thoughtful regarding sexual activity and explore the intentions behind our actions.

Now we move on to the positive things we can do to help our bodies thrive. Yoga Sutra 2.32 says that cleanliness, contentment, austerity, self-study, and devotion are the attitudes we must observe. They are called niyamas. As you read the list, can you see how they apply to your physical body as well as life in general?

Yogis of ancient times obsessed over cleanliness. There are stories of practitioners cleaning their intestines in disturbingly graphic ways. There are accounts of yogis taking their intestines out of their bodies, cleaning them, and putting them back again. We can debate whether that is a myth, but I have seen a teacher who was able to swallow a cloth and pass it through his whole digestive system. Amazing (or gross) as that might seem, it shows the length to which serious yogis will go to clean their digestive systems. I will share some less extreme, more gentle cleansing techniques later in this chapter.

Contentment is an attitude to aspire to, because when we are calm and balanced, our surroundings reflect that back to us and life is pleasant. But contentment is not easy to achieve and to that effect I offer guidance in the emotional body chapter.

Austerity doesn't just relate to money, nor does it mean starving or denying simple pleasures. It means being intelligent and focused in our lives and the way we use our resources.

Self-study is an important element of this book. We are examining our instincts, habits, emotions, actions, decisions, our past and present life conditions, and more. The best gift we can give ourselves and others is to understand our strengths and weaknesses and work on improving our ways, getting stronger, and building character.

Devotion, the last quality the Yoga Sutra lists, involves cultivating an attitude of surrender. Some schools of yoga claim that devotion is the fastest way to attain the state of yoga. That may be true, and for me, understanding that surrendering to the will of what I define as my personal Spirit, has been the most transformative step and the most positive one. We will talk more about devotion in the wisdom and spiritual body chapters. For now, I would like to return to cleanliness to offer ways in which you can think and look at how to cleanse your body and your immediate surroundings. I will move in order, from the top to the bottom of the body, and then move to cleaning our surroundings.

Yoga Cleansings

The physical yoga body is represented in the first chakra, which influences how we think of ourselves. The element of the physical body is earth, hence the grounding quality of its name, "root".

The root chakra contains everything related to our identities. For example, name, address, nationality, height, eye color, etc. The first chakra also relates to our physical characteristics, which, through yoga, we aim to free from impurities through practicing physical cleansing techniques.

Kapalabhati: Skull Cleansing

Kapalabhati is an excellent exercise for achieving clarity of mind. I consider it the most important breathing exercise. In the sixth class of the YouTube companion videos, we will practice and go over all the details, but it will be helpful for you to first read the instructions for a more comprehensive way of approaching it.

Kapalabhati is an exercise in exhaling. In the practice, you exhale forcefully through the nose. There is no need to force inhalation because it will happen naturally. The exhalation comes with a push from the lower belly onto the back of the spine. As the belly flaps, it awakens the second chakra. The second chakra holds creativity, and as you become aware of it, you will experience a sense of restful imagination. Your mind will feel clean and energized, and you may be inspired to follow your artistic vein. I love doing kapalabhati at the end of each class.

It's best to build your kapalabhati practice gradually. I suggest three cycles of ten repetitions to begin with, but as you build your practice and make it your own, you can add more repetitions and counts. The more you practice, the more you will be able to repeat and extend the cycles.

I enjoy kapalabhati because after a round of these forceful exhales, the last inhalation comes as sweet relief, relaxing all the muscles of the respiratory system. This relaxation, coupled with mental clarity, brings me as close to a state of bliss as I have ever experienced.

The Practice

- Check your inner state. Write down some words that describe your feelings.
- Sit on the floor with a straight back. Put a cushion under your butt so that your hips are slightly higher than your knees.
- If this is not possible, you can sit on a chair and put both feet on the floor.
- Put your palms on your lower belly, right below the belly button, so you can feel where the exhalations will originate.
- Exhale forcefully through the nose, without moving the spine or your body.
- Let the inhale happen naturally.
- Repeat for ten counts.
- Rest.
- Do two more cycles for a total of three.
- Take the resting pose.

- Write about how you feel. Is there any difference in your state of mind?

Cleaning the Tongue and Flossing

The number of individual bacteria in each of our mouths is roughly equal to the world's entire population. So how can we keep such a lively environment clean? When a dentist asks you to floss every day, you may roll your eyes, as did I, until I became familiar with these practices. I was advised to floss and use a tongue scraper daily. Without being too graphic, I recommend that you get a tongue scraper and try it so you can have a visceral reaction to what you see when you use it. I bet you never knew that a tongue could get that dirty.

Trataka: Cleansing the Optic Nerve

Our eyes are curious, they want to look, make out what things are, understand, and look again. They have a playful and fiery quality. The eyes are like unruly children. They can be all over the place and will name and judge things; they will incite the mind to create stories about what they take in. The eyes want to play, create forms, and engage with their surroundings. In today's world, the eyes are overstimulated and often get overwhelmed and exhausted. Trataka is defined as "gazing in a steady way." It is the exercise that gives the eyes a chance to rest and regenerate.

Think about your eyes for a moment and relax them. Take a breath and think about relaxing them a little more. Feel the millions of nerve fibers that carry visual messages from your retina to your brain. Send welcoming and warm energy to your optic nerve as you visualize it. Sensing the optic nerve should come naturally because it is very sensitive.

With the exercise of trataka, we give our optic functions a gentle massage and a dose of attention and love. As you practice, you will feel less tension in the forehead and eye sockets, and you may even notice sensation in the area of the inner third eye, the vortex through which you can perceive the world without looking. Over time, your eyes should begin to relax and shine.

The Practice

Trataka practice usually produces better results, and is more convenient, at night before bed. It may also help you fall asleep. Many practitioners relate vibrant dreams when they practice.

- Find a room where there is limited air circulation and make it as dark as possible.
- Light a candle and place it in front of you. Position the flame at the height of your eyes.
- See that the flame is as quiet as can be. You may need to close windows or doors that let wind come through.
- Watch the flame without blinking until your eyes water.
- When you feel moisture in your eyes and slight discomfort, put the candle out, close your eyes, and lay down.
- As an optional step, when you lay down, repeat the mantra "om" 27 times.
- Enjoy a good night's sleep.
- Write down your experiences and compare them over time.

Neti: Nostril Cleansing

Popularized through advertising promotions, the neti pot has become a household item. They are commonly used to clean pollution out of nostrils and to improve breathing. However, before incorporating one into your practice, make sure to test it out in a gentle way because for some, it can cause irritation of the nasal passages and sinuses. If this is your case, and as with any practice, the love of yoga should come first. Remember that if it hurts, it's not yoga. Suggestions for the most effective pot to use can be found in the resources section.

The Practice

- Check your mental and physical state before you practice.
- Write down a few words that describe how you are feeling.
- Fill a neti pot with warm water. Adding a pinch of salt is optional and may provide a more thorough cleansing.
- Stand over a sink.
- Tilt your head to the right and insert the neti pot spout into your left nostril.
- Don't force. Let the water run its course, respecting your body's response.
- The water will eventually flow out through the right nostril.
- Release the neti pot spout and come back to center.
- Tilt your head to the left and insert the neti pot spout into your right nostril.
- Let the water flow.
- Do a round of forceful exhaling to clear both nostrils when you finish.
- Journal about what you felt during and after the exercise.
- Take time to rest.

Dry Brushing

Our bodies accumulate dead cells that stick to the surface of our skin. Dry brushing clears these cells and allows our pores to breathe. The goal of dry brushing is to pamper your skin, not treat it harshly. It should be done in gentle circular motions and only once or twice a week. I particularly enjoy brushing thin areas of the body, like the lower legs, which tend to get dryer, especially in the winter.

There are many types of brushes. Bristles can be natural or synthetic and vary in thickness. I suggest starting with a soft brush that will treat your skin delicately and advancing to a thicker brush for more intense cleaning. I listed the brush I use in the resources section.

After you brush, use almond oil mixed with your favorite lotion to restore moisture to your skin.

Basti: Enemas

When I first heard that I would do coffee enemas while I was attending my teacher training, my first reaction was, "eww." I needed to hear more before I would even consider it, and the teacher understood this. He told us to laugh all we wanted and get our fears out in the open. Then we got down to business. I had always known that a clean digestive system was important for the body to function efficiently, but I didn't realize how seriously yogis address it. After learning that ancient yogis would sit in a river and perform enemas using bamboo shoots, a modern enema kit seemed less objectionable.

But why is this practice so important? The digestive system not only affects our physical energy levels, but is also integral in accessing higher states of spirituality. *The Hatha Yoga Pradipika* says that "basti" (enema) washes the bowels and removes excess bacteria, waste, and heat from the lower intestines. Beyond this, it helps in releasing spiritual energy. Consider the blossoming of the lotus flower as a metaphor for this spiritual energy. The lotus is rooted in mud, but it's energy travels upward through its stem, looking for light, where its beauty can blossom. We are rooted in a body that contains unclean elements, but when we cleanse, we can move upwards in our spiritual stem and blossom in the light.

The main obstacle to a clear body is a clogged digestive system. TK Krishnamacharya claims that all sickness originates in the stomach. Problems occur when there is a blockage somewhere in the transition between ingestion and elimination.

Many conditions affect your yoga practice and suitability to practice cleansing enemas. Consult a doctor who is familiar with your overall health and proceed with caution. Personally, I only consider an enema when more than forty-eight hours have elapsed without a bowel movement. Basti helps with irregularities, but is not a substitute for the natural movement of the intestines. If constipation persists, the problem is likely more significant. Consider learning and practicing this procedure with an experienced teacher who can guide you in person.

The Practice

You will need an enema bag or complete enema kit. It is important that the liquid you use is warm, but not too hot. I use a mix of cold water and watery warm drip coffee. If coffee is not your thing, use warm water only. I suggest doing the procedure in the morning and on an empty stomach.

Once you fill the bag, hang it so the liquid will flow down through the tube. Lay down on towels to stay warm. Remove the small end of the tube and insert it slightly and carefully into the rectum, no more than one and a half inches, and open the valve slowly, taking only as much liquid as you can and at a speed that doesn't cause pain.

The secret to a successful practice is to go slow. Let me repeat that, go slow, very slow. As the liquid comes in and fills the intestines, regulate the intensity and amount that goes in. Stop when the body has had enough, and rest before going further.

Once the intestines have taken as much liquid as they can, remain laying down for a few minutes if you can. When you feel that your body is ready to release, move to the toilet. Again, do not force. Let the liquid come out at a natural pace. Relax your muscles and let them do their work. You may feel the liquid moving around, and you can massage your stomach to facilitate elimination. A successful procedure will eliminate waste that has been accumulating in your intestines for days, months, or even years. Once you finish, lay in savasana and rest for at least fifteen minutes.

Spiritual House Cleaning

If you're familiar with the TV show *Hoarders*, you already know the discomfort you feel when you watch it. As in the case of all addictions, hoarders suffer from a spiritual disease, which keeps them isolated, in this case, behind barriers of junk. Our physical, mental, emotional, and spiritual cues are affected by our environment. An orderly home provides a state of harmony, while an untidy and messy space disrupts our comfort and our sense of well-being. A clean house is one that invites divine energies and all their manifestations. These may be wealth, love, or beauty. Monks live in pristine environments, and ashrams encourage guests to contribute to the meticulous upkeep of their grounds to provide a space where positive spiritual energies can flourish.

The Hatha Yoga Pradipika says that having a clean space is indispensable. Think about it, if you are expecting interesting and loving visitors, you will likely make your house clean and orderly. In the same way, inviting divine energy involves preparing and maintaining a space of cleanliness. Keeping your house clean is a spiritual job. A noisy, cluttered, and neglected space creates negative energy. In a messy home, the effort needed to ignore obstructions will divert energy and focus from your practice. Make time to keep your environment presentable even if it means occasionally skipping your asana practice. Creating a flow between inner and outer cleanliness makes life better.

An untidy home can affect my mood negatively. However, no matter how much I organize and clean, "stuff" still seems to accumulate. When the clutter starts to get out of hand and the prospect of a full house cleaning project seems overwhelming, I attack the mess a little at a time. Since yoga texts don't specify home cleaning strategies, I wanted to share the exercise that has helped me make home-keeping into a spiritual practice. The best part is it takes only ten minutes a day.

The Practice

For the next thirty days, dedicate ten minutes per day to focus on making your environment beautiful. Think of it as a ten-minute investment in your spiritual growth. A kitchen timer works well to count the minutes. Avoid using your phone as it will distract you. Before starting the timer, think about an area that could use some cleaning or organizing. Narrowing the project to a single pile of books or just one drawer makes it less intimidating. When the counter starts, immediately touch one of the things in that area. For example, if you are looking at shoes, touch one of them immediately. Connect with the task in a kinetic way, let it enter your system via touch. During the ten minutes, dedicate yourself entirely to the project. If your mind is reluctant, you can reassure it that you won't go past the allotted time. When the timer signals that time is up, let go of your task and stop. Just working for ten minutes per day for thirty days will show you the power of focused attention to your home. You can get better results if you journal daily to consider your progress and positive emotions. The beauty of this practice is that it creates a short ritual with positive results.

This exercise is not only practical, but deeply spiritual for me. I learned that when focusing on a specific task, with the restriction of a timer, I enter a state of being outside of time. I can carefully consider each object and decide to keep it or let it go. When I organized my jewelry box, for example, I found earrings that I knew I would never wear again because they stirred bad memories and emotions. After journaling, I returned to the project the next day and I felt an overwhelming need to transform the earrings into a new experience. I decided to sell them and use the money to go on a spiritual retreat. Ridding myself of the unhappy memories inspired a break from daily life, a trip to a lovely retreat and long walks in nature. Taking time to observe each step of the cleansing was more rewarding than doing it in a rush.

After only a week of this ten-minute practice, you will be surprised by how different things look. A little effort goes a long way when time has boundaries and you focus your energy. After a month, the change will be noticeable and you may be inspired to continue the practice.

Loving Yourself as a Cleansing Action

One of the most important precepts of yoga is that of loving yourself. It's also one of the hardest to learn. Many people are uncomfortable with the idea. How do you love yourself? There are simple ways in which you can express love and gratitude for your yoga body and spirit. You can get a massage if you're feeling tense. You can go to the dentist for a cleaning and keep annual check-ups with your doctor. You can take your inner child to a movie or a museum to let it play.

Write down ten things you would do if time and money were no object. For me, some would be taking a software design class, attending a silent retreat in Costa Rica, taking a week of intensive ping pong lessons, visiting a national park, having a facial, swimming, or taking a salsa class. What are yours? There are no bad ideas, just write what comes immediately to mind. These free-flowing wishes are telling, because they reveal areas in which you may need to add some fun and energy to your life.

Look at your list and pick your three favorites. Write them on a piece of paper and post it on your refrigerator as a reminder of your goals. If you find your wishes are too grand, you can still address the underlying desire. If you wrote that you want to visit temples in Japan, but that's not currently within your means, you can find a nearby exhibition of temples or visit a local Japanese community. You could print images of the temples you want to visit and make a collage. You can begin to expand your imagination in ways that nurture your soul. I may not be able to dedicate a full week to ping pong training, but I can enjoy an afternoon of playing at a local community center. There are always ways to create some of the energy that your body and soul are craving. By keeping your three wishes where you can see them, you'll get inspiration to nurture your passion.

I have also learned to avoid "HALT," an acronym for hungry, angry, lonely, tired. I like that it sounds like an order, which is how I treat it. If I don't HALT these, my body will suffer. When I was completing this book and creating the companion videos, I went without proper rest for weeks. One day, when I was editing text and planning the next video, I felt dizzy. I brushed it off as temporary, but the dizziness got worse until I couldn't read the words on the computer screen. I stood up to go to my bed and the whole room began to spin. I had to crawl on all fours, and even then, I barely made it. When I reached the bed, I called friends and with their help, I calmed down and made an appointment to see a doctor. My condition was diagnosed as vertigo, caused by an inner ear imbalance. The doctor mentioned that although the cause is not easy to identify, stress can play a role in triggering it. The metaphor of getting out of balance was not lost on me. I was tired and needed rest. I had been working too hard, and my body could not keep up. To avoid these hard life lessons, I've learned to use the acronym of HALT as a key element of daily living.

Sleep Hygiene

Without proper sleep, our bodies and minds won't function at their potential. Lack of sleep might indicate high-stress levels, a desire to cover up feelings, or a need to control things by staying awake. Letting go of negative thoughts will facilitate healthy sleep, as will a comfortable and calming environment.

The Practice

Your body doesn't just absorb light through the eyes, it also absorbs it through the skin, our largest organ. Before you go to bed create complete darkness in your room. Sleeping in a pitch-black bedroom encourages your whole body to rest. Set a cool temperature, sixty-eight degrees or lower. The body will feel comforted under the blankets in total darkness. Avoid screens or caffeine for at least three hours before you retire.

Affirmations for the Physical Yoga Body

- I love and respect myself.
- I treat my body with care.
- I use cleansing practices to relax and heal.
- My body is my temple.
- My home is in order.
- I let go of negativity.
- I understand that life is about progress, not perfection.

CHAPTER 2

The Breathing YOGA BODY

The breathing body is associated with the element of water because of its constant ebbs and flows. Just as the power of water is harnessed through the use of dams, we gather and increase the power of our breath by using yoga breathing techniques to channel and direct its energy. Yogis use an alternative word for breath, *prana*. Prana refers not only to breathing, but is the all-encompassing life force that we absorb from air. Prana regulates how much energy and vitality our bodies are able to store. It contains and preserves our life force. The more freely and efficiently we breathe, the more prana we possess. As we practice yoga, we learn to gather, store, and use our energy efficiently. As our access to life energy increases, we become better able to transform it into creativity. This transformation is the function of the second chakra, which works toward creating new life. We can use the second chakra in two ways: as a literal incarnation of life force (giving birth), or through expressing our talents and visions. The second chakra is intimately linked to the way we breathe because our expressions and creativity function optimally when our nervous system is in balance.

As our breathing and nervous system work in unison, our breath also connects us to our feelings. Think of when you are scared and your breath stops, or when you are anxious and you gasp or pant. If we improve the way we breathe, we can ease our nerves. And if we ease our nerves, we have a better chance of slowing down the mind and entering a state of meditation. In the previous chapter, we worked on cleansing our physical bodies and our environment. Now we focus on refining and improving our breathing to cleanse the nervous system.

The nervous system works closely with our glands and organs to maintain stable conditions for our bodies to function efficiently. It is also at the core of our mental activities. Ancient yoga texts suggest that to make all body functions healthy, we need only to focus on one. If one system is healthy, then the rest will follow. This phenomenon can be observed in both scientific and somatic systems. In one study, researchers observing a group of wall-hanging clocks found that sound pulses would travel through the wall from one clock to another, influencing their pendulums and causing them to synchronize. I have experienced a similar effect working in an office side-by-side with other women. After a few months, our menstrual cycles adjusted naturally and became synchronous. This chapter will concentrate on clearing the breath and strengthening the nervous system. The other systems will follow and synchronize in optimal health.

Your Breathing

Your personal way of breathing has developed over your lifetime and has become a pattern. That is neither good nor bad. It's just a fact. When you inhale, you take air into your lungs by using a set of muscles and movements in a manner that is unique to you. Every experience since birth has molded your way of breathing. These include positive and negative experiences, such as neglect or abuse, which can affect developing nervous systems and alter breathing patterns.

A yoga teacher I admire, Richard Freeman, says that yogis become "connoisseurs of the breath." I like this phrase because it makes me think of wine and how wine connoisseurs train their taste buds to detect flavors and subtleties of wine. In the same way, yogis observe all aspects of breathing. Look at some of the coarse ways we describe problems with our breathing:

- struggling to breathe
- breathing heavily
- out of breath
- panting
- choking
- laboring

As you become more attuned to the process, you may detect more refined flavors of breath. For example:

- smooth
- raspy
- long
- heated
- cool

Take this moment, for example, and observe your breathing. Can you describe it? Does it feel relaxed or shallow? Are your inhales and exhales long or short? Is one nostril more active than the other?

The first step to noticing the effects of breathing is awareness of the breathing cycle. Set a timer for one minute and count how many times you breathe. Count the full cycle of inhalation and exhalation as one. Beware of what the breath will do because when we are observing it, it may behave unnaturally. It might want to go slower or faster to show off. Just go along with it and keep the count. The average person breathes between twelve and fourteen times per minute. If you counted more or less than the average, don't worry, because awareness is the first step.

With practice, we will aim to refine this number to a suitable count and increase breathing efficiency.

Pranayama:
Breathing Extension and Control

The word pranayama has two parts, prana and ayama. Prana is the vital energy of the breath. Ayama means to control and extend. Through the practice of pranayama, we extend and control our life force. The four exercises we will practice in the sixth class will offer a way to become conscious of breathing during your asana practice, cleanse your mind, and balance your nervous system. You will gain awareness, clarity, and an attitude of serenity that comes with a balanced nervous system.

The sixth video companion class, called "Your Breath," is one you can practice every day. It is wonderful after asana practice in the morning, and it can also help you wind down after a long day. The breathing exercises will move you into a headspace of clarity. This class is powerful because it helps you absorb and retain precious life-giving energy. Whenever you need to calm your nervous system, regain your focus, or take a time out, hit play and get into it.

There are four techniques of breathing we will practice together. The first one, ujjayi breathing, is implicit in every asana practice and helps us pair movement to the flow of breathing. The second practice is a restorative exercise, oceanic breathing. Similar to waves steadily rolling up on the sand and then withdrawing back into the ocean, we will learn to create a calming rhythm of breath. We have already practiced the third exercise in the previous chapter. It is kapalabhati, or forceful exhalation. The fourth is a specific cleansing technique for the nervous system, Nadi Shodhana.

Ujjayi The Victorious Breath

How to Breathe When Practicing Asanas

We practice the victorious, ujjayi breath, together with our asanas, by making a sound. For this breathing technique, think of how Darth Vader breathes: slow and raspy.

We will use the victorious breath during our practice by creating a rhythm that synchronizes it to our movements. For example, we will be inhaling to an upward dog, exhaling to a downward dog, and so on. At first it may be difficult to incorporate the breathing elements, but the more you practice, the easier it will become. Follow the instruction and use the wisdom of your body to learn when to inhale and exhale. Slowly all the details will come together, and you will appreciate why it is called the victorious breath.

Benefits of the Ujjayi Breath

- warms up the body
- produces inner heat that helps release toxins
- makes us aware of our patterns of breath
- coordinates breath with movements
- elongates inhalations and exhalations
- revitalizes the body
- eases nervousness

A Word About "Breathing Deeply"

I don't recommend breathing deeply. Breathing deeply reminds me of my annual physical exam where the doctor puts a stethoscope on my back and asks me to take deep breaths. It is uncomfortable. Trying to repeatedly breathe deeply is counteractive and taxes the respiratory system. In the past, when yoga instructors asked me to breathe deeply, I became exhausted. Also, strenuous breathing fills up the thoracic cavity with air and can restrict movement.

Instead of the depth of breath, focus on length and quality. We want to feel that air is going evenly to all parts of the body. We want to have a smooth and fluid breath that reaches evenly across our lungs and becomes stable. Your breath has an intelligent rhythm of its own. When I ask you to do long inhales and long exhales during the video practices, know that they are reminders to look for quality and length, and find your rhythm. You are the one that will coordinate your movements to the flow and quality of your breathing.

Oceanic Breathing

This is probably the most relaxing and centering exercise I know. The waves we will generate by isolating each part of our breath will create a soothing and peaceful state. This calm and centered space is important for practices that will follow.

To begin, lay down on your back and bend your knees. Think of your torso as having three distinct parts. One is the belly, the area that goes from the pelvic floor up to the waist. If I ask you to breathe with your belly, visualize sending air only to the lower abdomen. You may find it difficult at first to completely isolate your breath to specific areas, and that is okay. Next, focus on the ribcage, the area that contains your sternum and ribs. Can you send air only to that area? Again, the goal is to develop an awareness of how breath flows throughout our bodies. Don't worry if your breathing is not perfectly isolated. Next imagine breathing with the ceiling of your chest, the area between the heart and the neck.

Now we can coordinate the three areas of the torso to create a wave of breathing. We'll do this by breaking down each inhalation and exhalation into three parts. As you inhale, first send air to the belly, then up to the ribcage and then the chest. Hold for three counts and then exhale from the chest, then down through the ribcage and the abdomen, then rest for one count. There is no need to hold the breath in each zone. Let it flow like a wave, inhaling up through your body and exhaling back down, with a welcome stop at the end of each cycle. You may find it helpful to put your hands on your belly and move them to the ribcage and to the chest as you breathe.

This exercise is helpful for falling asleep or quieting your mind. You will feel a relaxing effect and your body may even continue the rhythm after you're asleep. You'll wake up feeling rested and energized.

Kapalabhati: Skull Shining

You may have already practiced this exercise during the previous chapter when we talked about cleansings. If that is the case, you have a head start here.

The word kapalabhati has two parts, kapal, which means skull, and bhati, which means shining. You will feel the power of kapalabhati when you practice with the sixth video.

The Hatha Yoga Pradipika says that for kapalabhati we "perform exhalation and inhalation rapidly like the bellows of a blacksmith." Note that the teaching starts with exhalation. Kapalabhati starts in the middle of an exhale. When we exhale forcefully, the lower belly slaps the area of the sacrum, the second chakra. Then the inhalation happens without any thinking or straining. We allow it.

In the sixth video class, we will practice three rounds of twenty expulsions. If you get tired or lose your rhythm, it's okay to stop. Work at your own pace as it's best to build the repetitions slowly. If you practice daily, you may increase your stamina to twenty-five or thirty counts and increase the number of cycles.

Benefits of Kapalabhati

- clears the mind
- relieves stress
- increases metabolism
- increases concentration
- eases tension
- clears the mind and improves mood
- creates a feeling of bliss

Nadi Shodhana: Alternate Nostril Breathing

A remarkable discovery by ancient yogis is that breathing through a particular nostril affects the opposite side of the brain and its functions. The left nostril affects the right side of the brain and vice-versa. Think of it as cross wiring.

Breathing through the left nostril activates what yogis describe as the lunar channel of the body. The lunar passage awakens the right hemisphere of the brain and all its poetry. Comedian Bo Burnham suspects that if this artistic side of the brain could speak, it would say:

"I am the right brain, I have feelings. I'm a little all over the place, but I'm lustful, trustful, and I'm looking for somebody to love."

The right brain is curious, emotional, earthy, and suggests the feminine archetype. Breathing through the left nostril will awaken your creativity and emotional side. It can also wake you up from lethargy as it produces exciting and vivid ideas and visualizations.

Alternatively, when breathing through the right nostril, the sun passage becomes active, and the left brain lights up. The analytical archetype takes the reins with its practical, masculine energy.

Burnham describes it like this: "I am the left brain, I am the left brain. I work really hard 'til my inevitable death brain."

When we breathe through the right, sun-nostril, and wake up the left side of the brain, we are better able to make decisions and perform pragmatic tasks. We may plan the year, calculate taxes, concentrate on a tedious legal document, or create formulas in a spreadsheet.

During the writing of this chapter, I played with my breath by alternating nostrils. When I breathed only through the left nostril and activated my creative, right brain, I laughed and sang the lyrics I remembered from Bo Burnham. It was while in this state that I added his quotes describing brain functions. I found them both funny and illustrative. Later, my practical and analytical brain kicked in when I inhaled and exhaled through the right nostril. I calculated the effects of those quotes within a yoga book and made appropriate edits.

Knowing about these functions and how to control them has practical applications, an important aspect of a pranayama practice. Yogis investigate, practice, and measure results.

We can go beyond investigation and use this knowledge to quiet the mind and access deeper states of meditation. The interesting thing about meditation is that it's more successful when both sides of the brain work together, meaning when both nostrils are working simultaneously. In general, as we go through our day, one or the other of our nostrils will be imperceptibly more dominant. We may rarely find ourselves breathing through both equally. But, here and there, there is a moment in which both are active. At that time, and for a few moments, we are primed for deeper meditation. If we can re-create this balance while meditating, our chances for deeper experiences will improve. This is where the next practice comes into play. Nadi Shodhana is an alternating nostril breathing exercise. The name means nerve cleansing, and it is the final exercise in our class. When you prepare to practice along with the sixth video class, make sure your environment is calm and conducive to a meditative state.

How to Practice the Nerve Cleansing Breathing: Nadi Shodhana

- Sitting in a comfortable position with the spine straight, use your right thumb and ring finger to block each of your nostrils as instructed.
- Lightly block the left nostril with your ring finger.
- Breathe in through your right nostril for four counts.
- Simultaneously release your left nostril and block your right nostril with your thumb.
- Exhale through the left nostril for four counts.
- Repeat this cycle four times.
- Now block the right nostril with your thumb.
- Breathe in through your left nostril for four counts.
- Switch the fingers and exhale through the right nostril.
- Repeat this four times.

The Benefits

- relaxation
- preparation for meditation
- balancing activities of the brain
- calming of the nerves
- improved mood
- less anxiety
- overall well-being

At the end of this class we will practice a "bonus" breathing exercise to cool down the system. This breathing technique is called "Sheetali" and it will prepare you for a sweet after-practice relaxation.

Affirmations for the Breathing Yoga Body

- I focus on my breath.
- I cherish each breath.
- I notice how my breathing affects my mind.
- I practice asana with the victorious breath.
- I am conscious of which nostril is more active.
- My practice deepens when I add breath awareness.
- I am worthy of deeper states of consciousness.
- I meditate and reap the peace that comes with it.
- I use my practice and its fruits for the benefit of others.

CHAPTER 3

The Emotional
YOGA BODY

The emotional yoga body holds the key to self-love and compassion. However, it also presents a challenge because it holds our difficult emotions and blind spots. To heal, we must confront that which hurts and maddens us. We need to be willing to see and explore our shortcomings so we can transform them. When we do, we learn to accept and love ourselves first, and as a result, we are open to extend our love to others.

The element of the emotional yoga body is fire. Think about times in which you are furious, "see red," or feel a "burning rage." When we focus on cleansing destructive, heated emotions, we can quench their fire and transform them into compassion. In effect, we channel the fire of the third chakra and transcend it to the love of the fourth, heart chakra.

The third chakra, Manipura, is located at the navel and affects our willpower. It provides motivation to succeed: to get a job, find a home, create a family, acquire wealth, etc. But the power of the third chakra can be also be destructive. Things can backfire if we try to rule the world or pursue irrational fantasies and desires.

The most important insight of the emotional body is recognizing and accepting what we feel. Start by looking at the triggers that push you and make you vulnerable to creating drama. Are you hurting in your life? Is something making you sad? Is your self-esteem suffering? Are you in pain? These are important questions to think about.

I grew up thinking I had to hide my frustrations and anger because I might seem unhinged or crazy if I showed how I felt. That is nonsense. We feel what we feel independent of what anyone may think. We need to validate our feelings and give them a voice. We need to listen to them even if they seem childish because they hold secrets to our healing. That doesn't mean we are going to act them out. As we get to know our emotional make-up, we become free of reactivity and determine how we move forward from a place of strength.

Humans have an infinite number of emotions. In this chapter, we will focus on only two, the ones that lie at the root of most of our negative behaviors – anger and fear. Yoga traditions do not ignore the emotional body, but they give little direction on how to influence or control it. For example, in *The Yoga Sutras*, Patanjali says that we can control the fires of emotionality through meditation and yoga practice. *The Hatha Yoga Pradipika* offers only ways to meditate by controlling the functions of body and breath. *The Bhagavat Gita* offers the option of meditating and surrendering. I have practiced yoga for years, and I can tell you that meditating, practicing postures, and offering my devotion to a divine source is not enough. If I get mad to the point of lashing out, all the yoga practice in the world won't calm me. If I am truly angry, no amount of meditation can get me out of that state. If I am paralyzed by fear, I can offer it all to the Divine and practice asanas and control my breathing, but the underlying cause will remain untouched.

Since there is so little within yoga literature that deals with the emotional yoga body, I offer a time-tested and effective technique, that of putting a metaphorical mirror in front of ourselves and looking at our actions. When we take an inventory of our lives, we see ourselves clearly, perhaps for the first time. When we are willing to observe exactly what we do and the role we play in each situation where life goes awry, we can get to the root of our problems. When we feel negative emotions brewing, we can stop and take a moment to examine and identify what is being triggered within us. We can consider our feelings, observe them, and think about why they are so powerful. As we identify our feelings, they lose power, and we gain a better understanding of ourselves. We become better prepared to confront situations in the future so that we will have a choice in what we do, rather than be overtaken by triggers.

Admitting we have triggering points is the first step to transformation. Many times, our issues stem from traumatic events we experienced in our formative years. Scarring situations from childhood, for example, can be difficult to confront. For years, I did not want to admit that alcoholism and disfunction existed in my family, and I denied any type of abuse because I wanted to believe that I had been raised in a stable environment. Healing happens when we are willing to take the blinders off and see things as they are. Also, through sharing my experiences, I have found that others relate because trauma caused by negligence and abuse is not uncommon.

The invitation of the emotional yoga body is to become true to ourselves by recognizing anger and fear, and then learning to process and release it. By addressing our anger and fear, we allow the fire of the third chakra to burn away impurities. Once we confront our emotions, we will stop lashing out, acting out, and hurting ourselves and others. We will have the ability to act thoughtfully instead of reacting unconsciously.

I once attended a retreat at the ashram of Swami Radha in British Columbia. During the retreat, we not only practiced yoga poses but also developed our emotional yoga bodies. During asana practice, we would stop after each pose and reflect on how each one affected our state of mind. During the day, we helped around the ashram by cooking or cleaning. We chanted mantras and developed an attitude of devotion. If feelings of fear or anger popped up, we stopped, grabbed our journals, and recorded them. In the evenings, we sat in a circle and discussed the events of the day. Together, we learned to express and examine our emotions. The retreat was influential in convincing me that yoga was my path because it loosened me up, and I began to accept my imperfections with a compassionate eye.

It would be nice to have settings such as a retreat or private teachers dedicated to looking after our spiritual growth. Since that is not always practical, we can become field researchers and study our own spiritual development. The following exercises can help stop the avalanche of destruction that unacknowledged anger and fear can cause.

Anger

Unchecked anger is never a good thing. It can lead to rage, loss of self-control, and even violence. When a trigger is activated, results can be immediate and drastic. This type of reactivity is what Eckart Tolle calls the *pain body*. When activated, the pain body can cause us to lose control of our minds and actions.

Even in less extreme cases, anger can disrupt our lives. Years ago, someone stole my wallet, walked into a bank, and attempted to withdraw $4,000 from my account. Since the only identification the bank required was my driver's license, which the thief had, they gave them the money. The next morning, I checked my account and saw that my entire savings was gone, and I lost it! First, I went into shock, then became agitated, started mumbling, and eventually began screaming, "What the heck?! How can the bank give away my money so easily?!" I ran to the bank and made a huge scene. I screamed and cried and demanded my money back. The momentum of my anger led to a complete loss of control. Even after the bank took responsibility and restored my funds,

I felt emotionally drained by my outburst. It took several inventories of my feelings, sharing with friends, journaling, praying, and meditating in addition to my daily practice to get back to a place of peace. It took weeks to get back to serenity, all because I didn't initially address my anger.

Observing our anger is of utmost importance for the life of yoga. We need serenity and stillness as pre-requisites for higher levels of spiritual progress. Releasing anger starts by accepting and facing it. Instead of screaming an expletive or showing a finger, we can stop and think things through. While it's easy to say this when not in the heat of the moment, there are ways to deal effectively with anger such as removing ourselves from triggering situations.

After the bank returned the money to my account and I calmed down, I could see that I had played a part in the drama and had hurt myself to the point where I needed weeks to recover. Yes, I had a right to be mad, and I was justified in asking the bank to return my money. But everything I did to make my case could have been done with a different attitude.

In taking stock of my actions, I identified a trigger. When I was growing up, my family didn't have much money, and there were days when we went to bed without dinner. The fear of that happening again triggered an irrational response. Something within me needed reassurance that I wasn't going to starve again. My outburst was out of proportion and came from underlying insecurities.

Exercise to Release Anger

- Accept the anger.
- Consider why you are angry.
- Write down the first thing you think or feel regarding your anger. The act of writing down your thoughts lets the emotional puss out. It is cathartic.

- Recognize a situation in your past that may be triggering the anger. What was happening then?
- Write down the first thing that comes to mind. You may be able to identify the trigger because, as the saying goes, hysterical is historical.
- Once you have identified the trigger, share it with a trusted friend or family member who won't judge or criticize you. In other words, someone who can listen in stillness.
- Acknowledge and say a prayer for your inner child that may have been hurt in the past. You will feel a release.
- Notice your part in the anger. Are there reasons you are continuing the cycle?
- Write any additional emotions that surfaced during the exercise.

We release anger when we identify what triggered it, and then accept it and love ourselves for recognizing it. We can then see where the trigger is coming from and send love to our past self who was hurt when vulnerable and young. If we catch anger early, acknowledge and process it, we can avoid unconscious reactions to it.

Fear

During weekends, when I was a young girl, my parents would take me and my siblings to a cabin in the woods. The house was in poor condition, but the property had access to a river. It was paradise to me. Except for one afternoon, when I found myself in the outhouse, terrified, because my father was filled with rage. He was pacing back and forth, waiting for me to come out so he could punish me.

Earlier that day, while he was taking a siesta, I had taken the neighbor's old wooden boat for a ride. I loved floating on the river and the feeling of freedom it brought. I felt something I never had before a sense of agency, energy, and delight. My father, however, was not pleased with my little adventure, and when I came back, he chased me until I found refuge in the outhouse.

When the sun set, it got cold, and I knew I would have to head back to the main house. I remember surrendering and hoping it wouldn't be so bad. As I faced my father's wrath, I was overcome by physical sensations: the pain in my scalp as he grabbed me by the hair, the rash on my back as he dragged me over the grass, and the sting of his belt. After a while, he left me on the ground and went inside. I was tired of screaming by then, so I lay sobbing in the dark.

Something within me changed that day. I had been attacked on all fronts: emotionally, physically, mentally, and spiritually. That day I learned that the world could be unsafe and that those I relied on to care for me could turn hostile and violent. I also felt that I couldn't trust anyone, especially men. I didn't know it then, but my father's aggressive reaction would have long-lasting repercussions. For years, I tried to pretend that day never happened. I buried my feelings because I thought it was wrong to express anger or fear. I tended to fear men and was unable to create solid romantic relationships because of an unconscious fear of abuse.

After that experience, I became frightened of trusting my instincts and following my dreams. The fear was ingrained deep within my soul and my physical body. As a child, that fear served and protected me from further beatings. However, as an adult, it hindered self-actualization. For decades, I hid in jobs that paid the bills but did not nurture me. I avoided pursuing freedom or following the call of my vocation because I subconsciously felt I would be hurt if I did. In romantic relationships, I repeated destructive patterns. I picked emotionally unavailable men at best and physically abusive at worst. I wish I were the only one with a story like this, but I've spoken with hundreds of women and men in support groups, and my story pales in comparison to some that I've heard.

Examining the emotional yoga body is an invitation to investigate our fears. Consider questions such as: Who hurt you? What did they do to you? Did it make you feel less safe? Did you think less of yourself for it? Did it stop you from pursuing a dream? These questions address defense mechanisms we use to avoid negative consequences we imagine could follow. Take out your journal and answer each of them. Let your thoughts reveal your feelings and witness them without judging. Get them out of your head and onto the page.

Many meditation techniques teach addressing angry and fearful feelings by letting them go as if they were passing clouds in the sky. However, when difficult emotions are present, we need more guidance. In his book, The Trauma of Everyday Life, Buddhist teacher Mark Epstein writes, "emotional content needs a welcoming attitude. Otherwise, it will remain undigested, waiting to jump out at inopportune times." Increasingly, spiritual teachers are recognizing that merely sitting on a cushion and meditating is not enough to release powerful emotions of anger and fear. It is more effective to actively investigate these strong emotions with a welcoming attitude, write them down, and share them.

How to Release Fears

We can name fears and talk about them. Both naming and sharing them set us free. Fears have more power when they remain hidden. Secrecy fuels their existence.

Exercise to Release Fear

Take note of your emotional state before you do this exercise. Grab a pen and paper. Write:

I am afraid of _____

Now keep writing line after line, listing any fear that pops into your mind. Write in a stream of consciousness without overthinking. Don't consider the origin of your fears until you are done with your list.

Here is a list I wrote a few years ago:
- I am afraid of growing old.
- I am afraid I will never work doing what I love.
- I am afraid of getting fat.
- I am afraid I will never have an intimate relationship.
- I am afraid of people laughing at me.
- I am afraid of being a failure.
- I am afraid of being poor and not having a place to live.
- I am afraid of dying in agony.

Do you share any of my fears? I think many of them are common. Listing your fears will cause them to ease. With this exercise, you open a sacred door of vulnerability through which they will flow out. You may get even better results by sharing your fears with someone you trust. Choosing a person who can listen without judgement is important. Consider someone who can hold spiritual space without being dismissive or too eager to fix things by offering quick solutions.

As you work to release your fears, your self-doubt will transform into self-compassion, and you will feel a selfless desire to help others release their anger and fear. You will become the person who holds space for the benefit of others when they want to share their own resentments and fears. When we release anger and fear, we become truly compassionate to ourselves and others. We vibrate at a higher frequency, that of love, and our hearts open.

Arriving at the Fourth Chakra

The emotional body is so powerful that it affects two chakras. You have been working through the third when you observed your emotions. Congratulations on your progress so far. The fourth chakra is in the heart, and upon arrival at it, we feel loved. We feel the type of love we have wanted all along.

About a year ago, I was regularly attending a support group. Since it was the middle of the pandemic and in-person meetings were potentially dangerous, we were only meeting virtually. However, a man from the group invited us to his house, where he said we could meet outside, in a big circle with plenty of space, wearing masks. At the time, I was becoming increasingly paranoid and depressed. I had been isolated in my small apartment for too long, so when this person opened the doors to his home and his heart, I was excited. I wanted to be among people and feel human warmth again. I had already been working on the exercises to release resentment and fear, and I was comfortable sharing my feelings with this group. I knew nobody would judge me or try to tell me what to do. I wasn't sure exactly what I would share at the meeting, but I was excited to go.

When my turn came to speak, I decided I would share two things. One would be my gratitude to my guiding Spirit for something I already had, and the other would be something I needed and wanted to ask for. I thanked the Spirit for my health, my friends, and my family. Then, when I was about to ask for something I didn't have, an amazing thing happened. I realized that I was feeling loved. I felt how all the people in the group as well as my family and friends cared for me. I felt a sense of warmth. Almost involuntarily, as if the words came from deep within me, I said, "I feel loved. What else is there to want?" In that moment, my heart opened.

The heart chakra is accessible, but arriving at it is not a quest. It is a clearing. We are doing the work required to cleanse the body, breath, and emotions to let love in. The heart chakra is also where we feel the love of Spirit. Of course, life will present tricky situations, but when you trust in the love within, you can accept whatever comes your way. Once there, the world offers itself. We either find a loving partner, or enjoy living alone. We move toward doing work we love or start loving the work we do. Love is not dependent on others; nobody can make us happy. We are the only ones that can bring joy and a rewarding life, and we experience it when we feel the love of Spirit.

Affirmations for the Emotional Body

- I take responsibility for my emotions.
- I commit to a daily practice of assessing my behaviors.
- I commit to not hurting others.
- I love and respect myself.
- I look for balance.
- I am generous with myself and others.
- I am ready to receive all the good that life has to offer.

CHAPTER 4

The Wisdom YOGA BODY

If you are unsure of your life purpose, the wisdom yoga body has the answer. The spiritual work you do at this level will reveal your destiny and open the pathway to fulfilling it.

When we understand our purpose in life, we love life. When we find what author Julia Cameron calls our "vein of gold," our passion, we feel happy and content. Renowned yogi Gregor Maehle believes, "once you embody your divine purpose, hanging around in samsara is no problem anymore." Samsara can be interpreted as a continuous cycle of suffering, and although the Buddha says that "living is suffering," living doesn't feel so bad when we are doing what we love and affecting others in a positive way.

The element of the wisdom body is air. Just as air passes through wind instruments to produce beautiful music, divine energy flows through our bodies and out into the world. The chakra associated with this body is the fifth, which is located in the throat and represents our talents, voice, expression, and actions. We open our fifth chakra when we allow divine energy to run through us. When that happens, we are guided by that energy and become instruments of Spirit.

But how do we become instruments of the Divine? How do we reveal our life purpose? Ancient yoga texts provide few answers. Perhaps yogis who lived a long time ago took these matters for granted, or maybe life was less complicated. It may be that they could get in touch with their inner divinity easier than we can today. But we are no longer living in the time of the Buddha or Patanjali. They lived in a less populated world with less distractions. Since I am living in the present day, I seek more clarity, so I keep searching, looking not just to yoga but to all spiritual traditions.

It's liberating to know that, in yoga, we are not bound to be followers or restricted by scriptures. Yoga is a living tradition, handed down through the ages by practitioners who incorporated new ideas along the way. The practice of yoga and its techniques do not remain stagnant; they evolve and improve. That means that today, the advancement of yoga toward a more complete practice relies on us. We are the ones seeking what works for ourselves. My findings and the practices I suggest are influenced by previous generations but are not literal teachings dictated by their texts. If you are open to my ideas, it is likely that you resonate with being part of the advancement of yoga. I would say you are a pioneer looking for what works and what is true for you. If you are interested in learning about established traditions, as well as developing your own, you're just like me.

Through my journey into subtle levels of my own yoga body, I felt an explosion of love which I described in the previous chapter. But recognizing my purpose required more investigation. After doing the exercises that follow, I was inspired to write this book and create the companion videos. The idea seemed a bit ambitious at first. I would have to not only write, edit and design the book, but also organize the production videos, learn about cameras, lighting, video editing and other things that were new to me. I wasn't intimidated by any of this, though, because I knew that once I was with purpose, the Divine would guide me through the process. And so it did. Every time I needed help or inspiration, it seemed to fall in place. I wish you the same good fortune.

Grab your journal and think about this: If you could lead ten alternative lives, what would you do with them? Write all ten in a stream of consciousness. Don't overthink and don't stop until you get to ten. Some I listed are astronaut, Oscar winning actress, famous yoga teacher, ping pong champion, world traveler, president of Argentina, farmer, pilot, Beyoncé (yes, that is allowed), and Olympian.

Your list will show what you love doing and give you clues about hidden desires. For example, I had no idea I like to fly *that* much. From the ten lives you listed, pick three and think of one thing you can do this week that is in some way related to your choices. Then do it. Although I cannot magically become Beyoncé, I can watch one of her concerts or practice dancing for a few minutes each day or just sing along to her music in the shower. Look for the *feeling* these activities give you and try to recreate it. I may not stand a chance of becoming a ping pong champion, but I can watch instructional videos to improve my game and get the feeling of being the best. When you start paying attention to the little things you enjoy and get familiar with that feeling, you create momentum and channel it toward what makes your heart sing.

The question remains, if we have a general idea of the things we enjoy, why is it so hard to dedicate ourselves completely to them? The block comes from feelings of unworthiness. These feelings of doubt and shame stand in the way of accepting ourselves as shining stars.

Here is how Marianne Williamson interprets the wisdom yoga body in her book, *A Return to Love:*

"Our deepest fear is not that we are inadequate. Our deepest fear is that we are powerful beyond measure. It is our light, not our darkness that most frightens us. We ask ourselves, 'Who am I to be brilliant, gorgeous, talented, fabulous?' Actually, who are you not to be? You are a child of God. Your playing small does not serve the world. There is nothing enlightened about shrinking so that other people won't feel insecure around you. We are all meant to shine, as children do. We were born to make manifest the glory of God that is within us. It's not just in some of us; it's in everyone. And as we let our own light shine, we unconsciously give other people permission to do the same. As we are liberated from our own fear, our presence automatically liberates others."

When I read this, I understood that playing small is restricting. We offer more to the world when we encourage ourselves to be as powerful as we can, without fear of intimidating others. Allowing ourselves to be the most talented we can be is the spiritual journey. The best gift we can give ourselves is the self-esteem to pursue our destiny rather than make ourselves small for fear of not fitting in.

There are some common fears that create self-doubt: we think we are too old or too young, or the things we want to do have already been done. But these doubts are not valid. The way you express yourself and the things you have to offer are special and unique, and there will always be people who will appreciate you.

I am especially moved by the final sentence of Marianne's message. As we are liberated, we liberate others. We free ourselves completely when we accept our light, and in so doing, we enable those who are watching us to do the same. The immediate impact of this subtle body on those close to you is verifiable. You will see it. You will sense it. As you become a conduit of light so will those around you.

Finding Our Purpose

We realize our divine purpose by doing what we have been doing all along, removing blocks. In previous subtle bodies we released toxins from the body and emotional baggage from the heart. At the wisdom level, we release guilt and shame and clear the path for a life of purpose and meaning.

I get excited when I hear inspirational talks that encourage me to embrace my destiny, do the things I love, and play big. I think we all have a desire to follow our path, but often find it difficult to put that desire into practice. One thing that impedes us is holding on to guilt and shame. In the previous yoga body, we addressed triggers that make us react in unconscious ways. At the wisdom body, we'll learn to set ourselves free by forgiving ourselves, those we hurt, and those who hurt us.

Forgiving Ourselves

We can prepare to ask for self-forgiveness by making a list of the times we were unkind to ourselves. It took a week to write my list because I found it difficult to face all the irresponsible actions from my past. But with every memory came a sense of relief. It was as if my body and my soul sensed I was trying to recall all the times I had made bad choices so that the painful memories could be purged. I began to feel forgiveness even before I asked.

When I finished the list, I wrote a letter to myself with specific situations for which I wanted to say, "I am sorry." They covered damage to my body, my career, and my relationships. Here are a few that were included:

"I am sorry that I abused you with toxic substances."

"I am sorry I neglected your nutrition in the name of looking good."

"I am sorry I overworked you."

"I am sorry I didn't give you a chance to pursue work you loved."

"I am sorry I rushed into relationships with people who were unavailable and unable to give you love."

With the letter in hand, I prepared a ceremony to formalize my amends. I created a spiritual space by lighting candles and burning sage. I made an altar and sat down to meditate for a few minutes. When I felt relaxed, I opened the letter and read it out loud. Soon after I started reading, I felt a rush of energy from within my body which I can only describe as intense love. With every word I spoke, I felt as if my skin was embracing me, as if my flesh was hugging my bones. My body was forgiving me. The feeling was so powerful that I wrapped my arms around myself. I was hugging my body, and she was hugging me back. I savored that loving energy, and after a while, I said a prayer:

"Spirit, thank you for showing me the love that is within me. Thank you for the forgiveness and infinite love of my body. I promise to treat myself with love, compassion, dignity, and patience. I promise to listen to your direction and fulfill the life you would have me live. This is the body and mind you have granted me for the span of my life, and I commit to treating them as sacred."

The day of the ceremony I learned what it feels like to have self-esteem. Self-forgiveness grounded me in trust, and I felt worthy. It can be frightening to own our light because when we accept that we have a purpose, there is responsibility that comes with it. There is a temptation to stay small because it's easier to stay in the numbness of inertia than pursue our destiny.

Forgiving myself opened the door to accepting that I have talents to offer. I felt liberated from the lingering shame of past decisions. All previous life experiences had prepared me for this moment, and I was finally accepting that I am amazing.

The same can happen for you. Through this ceremony, you can remove obstacles that block you from seeing your purpose clearly. You will see that you possess a marvelous mix of life experiences that make you unique. You make art by the way you live. You have a personal flair for living life, and you have knowledge that no one else has. You are a precious work of art.

Self-Forgiveness Ceremony

Start by journaling all the times you've caused harm to your body, your mind, and your soul. Include the things you regret not having done. Be careful not to judge or blame. Write everything that comes to mind.

Once your list is ready, write a letter to yourself with all the things you would like to say. Prepare a sacred space for your self-forgiveness ceremony. You can create a soft and loving environment with candles, incense, photos, and anything that inspires you. Sit down in silence and meditate for a few minutes, then open your letter, and read it aloud. Don't rush this part. Let your body feel the apology and express itself in its unique way. It is important to respect any response, including no answer at all. Making amends to yourself will always have an impact, but it will happen in its own time.

When you feel ready, offer a prayer of your own thoughts, promising never to hurt yourself again in any way. Promise your body that you will respect and honor it, and then close your ceremony.

Asking Forgiveness

Living our life purpose involves addressing our relationships with others. Just as the fulfillment of our life purpose includes helping, teaching, entertaining, or inspiring those around us, it is also dependent on how we treat them. To clear the path to our destiny, we must consider not only how our past actions have affected ourselves, but also how they have affected others.

When we make amends, we release guilt and shame and bring dignity to our purpose. By reflecting on how we have hurt others, we gain insight to how we can influence and inspire them. When we are willing to listen to how our actions have affected others, we are showing the courage it takes to address our faults and to change for the better. When we channel our divine work, we can transform the lives of others in a positive way.

The Wrong Way to Atone

In the plot of the TV show *Shameless*, Fiona is happy to be marrying the man she loves. Sean, the groom, ruins the wedding ceremony because he is high on drugs. A year after they break-up, Sean asks Fiona to meet. He intends to make amends but leaves the reason for the meeting vague. Fiona still has feelings for him and starts fantasizing about giving the relationship another chance. But Sean has since married someone else and only wants to apologize to clear his own conscience. He is not interested in facing the consequences of his actions. He just wants to smooth things over with a quick and insincere apology. Without giving her a chance to speak, he offers her a stack of money as restitution for the ruined wedding. Fiona is furious and throws the money back in Sean's face.

This scenario shows how making amends can go very wrong. Sean's first mistake was not telling Fiona why he wanted to see her, which would have given her the opportunity to decline. Also, he had no intention of revisiting the emotional damage he caused or offering a genuine apology. This is the wrong way of offering amends.

The Right Way to Make Amends

Consider this ritual.

1. Write down things you did that have affected someone negatively.
2. Make sure you are ready to hear the consequences of your actions.
3. Contact the person you hurt and ask them if they would be willing to hear an apology. If they decline, respect their wish and do a "living amends" instead. This is done by praying and committing to not repeating those actions.
4. If the person agrees, set a place and time to have a private conversation.
5. When you meet, tell the person what you feel you did wrong.
6. Gently ask them if they can tell you how your actions made them feel. Be tolerant and listen. Don't interrupt or correct them. Through listening, you will get a clearer view of yourself and the results of your actions. You can feel genuine remorse only after you are able to consider their feelings.
7. Tell them you are truly sorry.
8. Listen to what they say after you apologize. Let them talk. There may be more they want to share.
9. Ask them what you can do to remedy the mistake. Instead of offering some pre-determined restitution, give them a chance to tell you what they think is appropriate.
10. Provide the requested restitution if you can, or ask for time to consider if you're not sure. If you are uncomfortable or unable to meet their request, offer a thoughtful compromise. For example, if you don't have the means to repay a monetary debt in a lump sum, offer to repay in installments. Do what you can.

Revealing Your Life Purpose

When I was approaching this chapter, I had doubts about sharing the final step that led to discovering my own life purpose. After consulting with colleagues and considerable reflection, I decided it was necessary. The reason I was initially hesitant was because it involves an emotional exercise that asks us to stretch the limits of tolerance and forgiveness.

Genuine heartfelt forgiveness is sometimes difficult. This presents a problem, because the final obstacle to connecting with our purpose is releasing those who hurt us. By freeing them, we free ourselves.

I had great difficulty forgiving my father for years of neglect and mistreatment. One day, a teacher suggested that I ask *him*, my father, to forgive *me*. Not in person, but metaphorically. My first reaction was that this was ridiculous. There was no way I would say I'm sorry to him! Even if the apology could now only be extended beyond the grave, I would not even consider it. I would not expect anyone to apologize to someone who hurt them under any circumstance. Still, I continued to think about the suggestion until something interesting happened. I decided to approach the idea as a koan.

Zen Buddhists use koans to help them unravel greater truths. Koans are riddles or questions that have no clear answer, such as, *If a tree falls in a forest and no one is around to hear it, does it make a sound?* Their purpose is to shake us out of our common way of thinking and consider all possible answers.

Koans have an element of perplexity and aim to redirect the mind's momentum. That is exactly what happened to me. My teacher's suggestion outraged me at first, and then somehow re-wired my brain into looking at things from another perspective. Knowing that I had no need or inclination to apologize to someone who hurt me, I thought of it in a detached and hypothetical way. If I was to make such an apology, what would I even say?

And that's when it hit me. I could direct the apology to myself for holding on to the "story of my father." I could say I was sorry that I used painful memories of my father to keep me small, to keep me from reaching my potential because I had been hurt. I could say I am sorry to myself for blaming my father instead of looking at what I could do to change my circumstances. I could see that I had been hanging on to the feeling that I would always be the victim and used this as a crutch to seek compassion from others and to avoid owning my own behavior. Talk about a wakeup call.

There is no denying that many of us have unresolved pain from being hurt by others. The point of this exercise is not necessarily to heal that damage. The point is to challenge the ways in which we see our pain and consider if we are letting it (or the person that hurt us) hold power over us. We can then let go of the story that keeps us in victim mode.

Answer the following questions. Don't overthink it, just put pen to paper and record your thoughts.

- Is there a painful story from your past that you keep repeating?
- Do you have the same feelings every time you relive it?
- Do you expect a specific response from others when you retell this story?
- What do you gain from holding on to the story?

Stories of past trauma block us from our purpose when we give them power. We live in the gloom of their shadow instead of acting toward the light we love. Think about it, are there stories that hold power over you? Do they define you? Do they give you an excuse to hide from life?

Letting go of my biggest resentments by repeating this exercise inspired me to write this book. Free from feeling like a victim, I realized I could change the course of my own life by taking responsibility for my actions and not blaming ghosts.

Take a moment to appreciate the courageous work you have done to this point. Reflect on the insights you have had. As you move forward, pay close attention to your feelings and continue to journal. Your subtle bodies have been transforming and will need time to adjust.

Affirmations for the Wisdom Yoga Body

- I forgive myself.
- I learn from past mistakes.
- I am willing to be loving and compassionate.
- I make amends where appropriate.
- I am respectful of others.
- I speak clearly.
- I let go of victimhood and take responsibility for my current circumstances.
- I let divine energy run through me.
- I listen to divine inspiration and set goals to move forward.
- I listen to my intuition.
- I am willing to be a channel of light.

CHAPTER 5

The Spiritual YOGA BODY

The spiritual yoga body is joy. Feeling loved and doing what we love while seeing others benefit are the rewards for the spiritual work we do. As Gregor Maehle says, "There is no greater thrill than to feel oneself become a conduit of cosmic intelligence touching and transforming the life of others." We arrive at this subtle body when we offer our gifts, as directed by the Divine, without expecting anything in return. At this level, our subtle bodies will be in tune, and we will experience synchronicities and coincidences that sometimes feel like miracles.

One of the chakras associated with the spiritual yoga body is the sixth. This chakra, located in the forehead, awakens our ability to perceive what we cannot see with the naked eye. Through this intuitive way of seeing, we get a better understanding of what is happening around us, and we become better able to discriminate between fantasy and reality. The seventh chakra, which also belongs to the spiritual body, is something we can sense, but not grasp. When the seventh chakra opens, we no longer fear anything or desire anything. We don't even think. We are completely free from the tyranny of our conditioning, and we act solely from Divine direction. But this is not a state we can "obtain," it is something that happens organically. The seventh chakra opens when all the others are working together. It also requires surrendering completely to the process without trying to exert our own will.

The element of the spiritual yoga body is space. Science tells us that every human being is made of atoms, and atoms are 99% space. If we remove all the empty space from every person in the world and measure what is left, our aggregate volume would be smaller than that of a sugar cube. At the spiritual yoga body, we sense that what we are is not matter, but consciousness. We are one being, one awareness, which manifests as different individual creations. Space is also a metaphor. In spiritual talk, we speak of "holding space," or being a receptacle in which others can express themselves while we remain nonjudgmental witnesses. A good sign that you are thriving within the spiritual yoga body is that you can hear others without trying to impose your views and without telling them what to do. If you have this intensity of listening, should the person ask for feedback, you may surprise yourself with an unexpected answer, an original thought. At that moment, you will be speaking from the power of Spirit.

Exercise: Listening

- The next time someone is sharing an experience or their thoughts with you, open all your senses. Become the presence and the space.
- Listen to every word they say and let them speak without interruption. If you get ideas or an urge to share how what they're saying relates to your own life, let those thoughts go and continue to listen.
- After they finish, stay silent, even if this creates an air of discomfort. Allow yourself to experience something new, together with the other person. You are now holding space.

- If the person asks for feedback, then think about your response and offer it. If they don't, respect that.

When you are holding space, you surrender to the natural course of a conversation rather than trying to control it. If you become anxious and interrupt every time the person you're talking to mentions something you can relate to or have an opinion about, you make the conversation about yourself instead of holding space for them. Another important aspect of listening is overcoming the resistance to leaving silent pauses within a conversation merely because those pauses can feel uncomfortable. It's okay to let the conversation breathe. When you become a listening presence, something special happens: the person speaking, the Divine, and you, become one. The act of listening in a transparent way invites the power of Spirit to enter.

As you get acquainted with the listening exercise, you will notice that people feel attracted to your energy because they feel heard and understood. By providing space, you open a metaphorical room within which others can be with their own thoughts. They will often resolve their own issues if you merely listen and provide a few questions or comments to keep them on track. When you can provide a presence for someone and they are able to find their own solution to a problem, you will both feel satisfied.

If the person you are talking to asks for your opinion, take a moment before you speak to leave room for Divine insights. Whatever happens within the conversation, let it be. Don't judge the other person, the impact of the interaction, or yourself. A friend once related her dating frustrations and asked for my advice. I listened, asked questions, and offered my view. A short time later, she told me her dating life had greatly improved because of a revelation she had. Her new insight, word for word, was what I had shared in our earlier conversation. She said it as if it had been her idea all along. And in a way, it was. When we are connected to our Divinity and holding space, a common consciousness is created. It belongs to all of us.

Living Life on a Divine Level

Albert Einstein described the essence of the spiritual yoga body when he said, "I want to know God's thoughts. The rest are details." At the spiritual level, we have a new partner. It is a Divine energy that is playful, sweet, and caring. Whenever in doubt, we can ask for guidance. What should I wear today? What should I do? What should I write about? Should I marry this person? Is this a good job for me? No question is too vain or silly. After each request, we listen, and believe that the answers will come. My own source of Divine energy has a sense of humor. It speaks to me through other people, coincidences, or even conversations I overhear.

In the spiritual yoga body, we cultivate an intelligent passivity. Consider the saying, "Don't just do something, sit there." Instead of rushing around, trying to figure things out from a limited perspective, trust your access to universal wisdom and use your daily practice as an anchor for making better decisions. Follow what you hear in the intimacy of your relationship with your Spirit. Whatever path you follow will have meaning because you will be guided by infinite wisdom.

Synchronicity

Your inner connection to a Divine source will result in synchronicities and coincidences that might perplex you. When I am connected to my practices, I experience coincidences all the time. They are sometimes so remarkable that they are hard to believe.

One cold winter, I woke up to freezing water falling on my face. There had been a blizzard and snow from the roof was dripping through the ceiling and into my bedroom. By noon, the bedroom was a disaster. I had moved the mattress to the kitchen and turned the bed frame on its side, the carpet was soaking wet, and two ceiling panels had crashed to the floor. I was angry. My landlord did not seem to grasp the urgency of the situation or just didn't care. He said it would take at least a week to replace the ceiling and wouldn't even address the inevitable buildup of mold.

I had been living in that apartment building for four years. In that time, the landlord neglected necessary maintenance, never cleaned common areas, and had allowed the building to fall into disrepair. I think I only stayed because deep inside I didn't believe I deserved better. But this was the last straw, I could not fix this, and I didn't have the energy to argue about it. I was tired of the neglect, the dirt, the ants, the noise, the lack of light, and now this. I was done.

I got down on my knees and prayed for guidance. Why wasn't I in a place where I could feel safe? Why wasn't my Spirit helping me? What did I need to understand? Despite my distress, I found some relief through praying. And then I had an intuition. I heard a voice say, "wash away your tears and start looking for a new apartment." I washed my face and decided to have a little talk with this voice. "I won't settle," I said. "I won't compromise. I want a nice place to live, and if you are real, then you better come through for me." I asked to find a clean home with light, plenty of space, and wooden floors for my practice. I said that I would start the search, but He had to take care of the big picture. I told him how angry and sad I was. I told him everything.

I found five listings in the town I wanted to move to. Four of them had photos, but I didn't like any of them. The last one had no photos, but the description was perfect: top floor, well-kept building, wooden floors, laundry, located in the heart of the little town I loved, near the train.

I was able to make an appointment to see it the next day and when the realtor opened the door, I was blinded by light. It had a balcony and lots of direct sun. The apartment was clean, had lots of space, and the floors were perfect for yoga practice. Everything felt right. That same afternoon, I filled out an application and was approved. Then, only six days after I woke up to water dripping on my face at the old apartment, I had moved in and was ready to start life in my fabulous new home. And it was my birthday!

The number of things that had to line up for my move to happen so quickly was miraculous. I consider it a reward for living a spiritual practice. When we connect with our Divine supply of energy, we invite good things happen. Synchronicities like this are not unusual within the spiritual yoga body. You can expect them. When your energy matches that of what your Spirit wants to manifest through you, the doors of good fortune will open.

Meditation

If you already have a personal meditation or contemplation practice, keep it going. All practices will produce positive results and gain momentum when you attend to them over time. If you have not established a meditation routine, you can start with a simple one that works for me. When I wake up, I ask the Divine to guide my thoughts and direct my actions. I know that the concerns of the day will quickly flood my mind, so I have trained myself to address my spiritual guide the instant I wake up. I then prepare a cup of tea or coffee and sit in silence. I sit on my favorite couch with my posture as straight as possible. It's not an elaborate routine. I just allow myself to be in that space of stillness. These few quiet moments provide me the clarity I need to face the day.

I initially had to overcome a resistance to starting meditation practice, so I created a prayer to ask for help. You may find it will help you get started, or you may be inspired to create a prayer of your own.

Dear Spirit,
I have a resistance to enter the stillness of meditation
I know that this disconnects me from hearing your will
Help me, please, for I only have human strength
Show me, in ways I can understand, how you care for me and love me
Teach me how to be kind to myself and others
Let me feel your call and direction
I surrender to you
Amen.

My Spiritual Awakening

I had a mild spiritual awakening when I realized that my Spirit is mine and mine alone. Hear me out. In the past, I had the idea that if a Divine source loved me and spent time looking after me, it would take away love and attention from other, less fortunate, people. This was constrictive, limited thinking based on the belief that there is only one pie with a limited number of slices to feed everyone. But then I realized that the abundance of the universe is infinite. We all have our own, private source of Divinity to guide us. We should not feel selfish or fear robbing others of their light by focusing on ourselves.

Everyone can establish a personal partnership with the Divine. To test this, list three questions you have today. They can be anything. For example:

Spirit,
Who should I talk to today?
What should I wear?
What time should I go to sleep?

If you have more profound questions, your Spirit is ready and willing to answer those as well. The Course in Miracles says that there is no order of difficulty in miracles, so go ahead and ask for big things too. On a cheeky note, I believe that Spirit responds faster to first-time callers, so, if you have never done this before, ask away and see what happens.

A Spirit Box

I have a beautifully carved wooden box that I keep on an altar. It was a gift from my favorite uncle, so it has a special energy for me. Whenever I'm facing a dilemma or have an important question, I write it down and put the note it in the box. When loved ones have needs, I pray for their well-being and put their requests in the box. When I connect with readers of my newsletter and they send requests, I put them in there too. This action provides an immediate psychological relief. It releases (or at least reduces) the burden I am addressing, and it feels natural to put prayers in the hands of a force more powerful than myself.

I can't fully explain why this works so well, but it does. Try it for yourself. Look for your own Spirit box. It can be one you inherited that has meaning to you, or it can be something you find at a flea market or craft store. You can simply use a shoebox and add some decorations. Make sure the box you choose has your energy and your love in it.

When you have a question or a petition:
• Write it down.
• Be creative by adding a personal touch to your note. Maybe decorate it with stickers or colorful ink.
• Place it in the box and release it into the hands of the Divine.
• Let it be.

Looking back at letters I have written, I see how all the things I asked for received an answer. Sometimes the answers were direct, sometimes less obvious, and sometimes unexpected. One instance involved a friend who told me she was dejected because her career had not taken off as she had hoped. I wrote a prayer that her professional life would improve and put it in the box. A couple months later, we met for lunch and before I could even ask about her career, she said things had really turned around since she was profiled in a respected magazine as one of the most accomplished people in her field. When she showed me a copy of the article, I privately gave a wink of thanks to my Spirit.

Chanting Om

Yoga Sutra 1.27 states that the expression of the "One" is the sacred syllable om, meaning that if we could give a sound to the ultimate state of yoga, it would be *om*.

The Mundaka Upanishad, a sacred text of Indian philosophy, says that *om* is a bow, we are the arrow, and the state of yoga is the target. Constant meditation on the syllable *om* purifies the mind and helps us abandon destructive thoughts.

Repetition of *om* creates an atmosphere of devotion. The chant is centuries old and infused with the power of all the practitioners that have sung it before us. Think of it as a timeless, universal prayer. Repeating the syllable can also empower your vision for your future. You can chant *om* as you write your goals, when you ask for guidance, or as you put a note in your Spirit box. You can chant *om* as a healing prayer for loved ones, or simply to quiet your mind.

Remember when I mentioned my first yoga class, the one I took decades ago? That day, when the teacher asked us to sing *om* three times before we started the class, I was skeptical, and I didn't want to do it. But perhaps out of wanting to fit in, I gave it a try and by the third time I sang om, my disposition toward the practice started to change. I was on my way to shaping my yoga body.

Affirmations for the Spiritual Yoga Body

- I live by spiritual principles.
- I surrender to the Divine.
- I attend to my practice every day.
- I am aware of my actions.
- I accept miracles.
- My life is abundant.
- My work is meaningful.

Guide to
THE COMPANION CLASSES

The companion classes are designed to help you embody the knowledge and practices that are explored throughout the book. The first five classes correspond to the first chapter; the physical yoga body. Classes six through nine correspond to the remaining four bodies: breathing, emotional, wisdom, and spiritual. They focus on individual asanas that affect specifics of breathing, emotional release, access to wisdom, and spiritual development. Class ten represents the culmination of all the work you have done. This final class contains a comprehensive sequence of poses that engage all aspects of the yoga body. It is a sequence you can practice anywhere, keeping in mind that it will have a deeper effect if you have gone through the first nine classes, and gained a broader understanding of each part of the course.

In my personal practice, I follow a routine with the same structure as that of class ten. If you want to explore more intense asanas and challenges, I invite you to follow my other YouTube classes to continue your journey into the heart of yoga. But for now, it's time for you to reap the benefits of all your hard work and make the practice your own.

Use this guide as a reference together with the companion videos.

The companion videos can be found in a playlist on my YouTube channel: www.YouTube.com/c/ClaudiaAzula

Class 1: Sun Salutations

The focus of the first class is on warming up your body and synchronizing breathing to movements. Using the victorious, ujjayi breath, which we discussed in chapter one, you will have an opportunity to prepare your body, open it up, and let it flow easily from one asana to the next.

Reading the detailed steps of the sun salutations will help you understand the fine points of the movements and how they connect with each inhalation and exhalation. Observe the photographs and read the steps to gain an advantage in your practice.

Even on days when you don't have the necessary time or motivation for a lengthy yoga session, this short sequence will suffice to keep you active and focused.

Sun Salutation A

- Stand in mountain pose with feet together.
- Inhale using the ujjayi breath, raise your arms, and look up.
- Exhale and fold down into a forward bend.
- Inhale, straighten your back so it's parallel to the floor, and gaze forward.
- Exhale, place your palms (or fingertips) on the mat in front of you, and walk your feet back to plank pose.
- With the next inhalation, roll your feet over to upward facing dog, and then exhale and roll your feet over again, for downward facing dog.
- Hold here for five ujjayi breaths. Focus on elongating the inhale and the exhale so they take about the same amount of time.
- With the end of the fifth exhale look forward and walk your feet forward.
- Inhale putting your fingertips on the mat and straighten your back parallel to the ground. Exhale and fold forward.
- Inhale and come up slowly, raise your arms over your head, and

exhale as you lower your arms beside your torso.
- As you arrive in mountain pose, take a resting breath.

Repeat the sun salutation "A" two more times, for a total of three rounds.

Sun Salutation B

- Stand in mountain pose with feet together.
- Inhale, bend your knees slightly, raise your arms, and look up.
- Exhale, straighten your legs, and move into a forward bend.
- Inhale, straighten your back, and look forward.
- Exhale, place your palms (or fingertips) on the mat in front of you, and walk your feet back to plank pose.
- Inhale, roll your feet over for upward facing dog and then exhale and roll your feet over again, for downward facing dog.
- Bend your left foot about thirty degrees from the center line and bring your right foot forward in between your palms, for a lunge. Check to see that your heels are on the same line. Square your hips. Inhale and raise your arms for warrior 1. Then, on the exhale, place your palms next to your right leg and bring it back for plank pose.
- Roll your feet over for upward facing dog and roll them back for downward facing dog.
- Now, bend your right foot about thirty degrees from the center line. Bring the left foot forward in between your palms, for a lunge. Inhale and raise your arms. Then, on the exhale, place your palms next to your left leg and bring this leg back for plank.
- Inhale and roll your feet over for upward facing dog and exhale to roll them back for downward facing dog.
- Stay in downward facing dog for five breaths. Remember the ujjayi breath and feel how it begins to warm up the body.
- With the end of the fifth exhale look forward and walk your feet forward.
- Inhale and straighten your back parallel to the ground.
- Exhale and fold into a forward bend.
- Inhale, bend your knees, come up, and raise your arms. Exhale and straighten your legs while floating the arms back down for mountain pose.

Repeat the sun salutation "B" two more times, for a total of three rounds.

Reflections and Insights

Body sensations I noticed:

Changes in my breathing:

Emotional release:

Insights from my wisdom body:

Spiritual connection:

Class 2: Strength

The second class focuses on strengthening the structure of the physical body. We will explore postures like Utthita Trikonasana (triangle pose), and Parivrtta Trikonasana (extended triangle pose).

Utthita Trikonasana

The benefits of these postures include a regained sense of stability, correction of any imbalances in how you walk, and elongation of the spine. These postures also offer a deep stretch for the sides of the body, an area often neglected.

Parivrtta Trikonasana

Reflections and Insights

Body sensations I noticed:

Changes in my breathing:

Emotional release:

Insights from my wisdom body:

Spiritual connection:

Class 3: Balance

In one of the most fun classes, you will test your ability to stand on one leg. Balancing poses are enjoyable because the focus required does not allow us to be distracted by any negative thoughts. You will enjoy postures like Parsvottanasana (reversed prayer side triangle), and Dekasana (airplane pose).

Parsvottanasana

The benefits of these postures include improved balance (both on and off the mat), a deep stretching of the legs, hip stabilization, relief of back pressure, and toning of the core.

Dekasana

Reflections and Insights

Body sensations I noticed:

Changes in my breathing:

Emotional release:

Insights from my wisdom body:

Spiritual connection:

Class 4: Internal Cleansings

The gentle inner cleansing techniques of this class help to calibrate the internal organs. They will also bring more awareness when it comes to what and when you eat. You will get acquainted with how your vital organs respond when you awaken them gently. This class is great for constipation and to relieve tension and anxiety.

We will explore postures like Revolved Paschimottanasana (twisted forward bend), Marichyasana C, and Ardha Matsyendrasana, both of which are seated twists.

An additional benefit of this class is that it will result in good posture and better mobility.

Revolved Paschimottanasana

Maricyhasana C

Ardha Matsyendrasana

Reflections and Insights

Body sensations I noticed:

Changes in my breathing:

Emotional release:

Insights from my wisdom body:

Spiritual connection:

Class 5: Hip Openers

Hip openers have the side effect of opening emotional blocks and releasing psychological tension. They are like a physical representation of talk therapy.

We will work on: Janu Sirsasana (head to knee forward bending pose), Baddha Konasana (binded angle forward bend), and Upavishta Konasana (wide angle seated forward bend).

In addition to relieving emotional tension, all three of these postures open the hips, stretch the inner thighs, tone the supportive muscles around the lower back, and calm the nervous system.

Janu Sirsasana

Baddha Konasana

Upavishta Konasana

Reflections and Insights

Body sensations I noticed:

Changes in my breathing:

Emotional release:

Insights from my wisdom body:

Spiritual connection:

Class 6: Breathing Exercises

In this class, we will use simple and profound pranayama practices that will immediately bring you visible and tangible benefits. After you practice this class, you will have a more focused and centered disposition, and an attitude of receptivity.

We will start by laying down, with the Oceanic Breathing exercise. Then, we will sit in a comfortable position for Kapalabhati (skull shining), to clarify the mind. Next, we will perform Nadi Shodhana (alternate nostril breathing), and finish with a cooling exercise called Sheetali.

Nadi Shodhana

The benefits of these practices include clarity of mind, a reset of the nervous system, and a sense of serenity.

Sheetali

Reflections and Insights

Body sensations I noticed:

Changes in my breathing:

Emotional release:

Insights from my wisdom body:

Spiritual connection:

Class 7: Opening the Heart

The postures of this class are the physical representation of the influx of love that opening the heart chakra produces. We talked at length about how to open the heart in the emotional yoga body chapter. Now it's time to embody this profound sense of love and compassion.

The postures in this class include Bhujangasana (cobra), Dhanurasana (bow), and Urdhva Dhanurasana (wheel pose).

In addition to helping open the heart chakra, these poses improve posture and tone the muscles around the spine.

Bhujangasana

Dhanurasana

Urdhva Dhanurasana

Reflections and Insights

Body sensations I noticed:

Changes in my breathing:

Emotional release:

Insights from my wisdom body:

Spiritual connection:

Class 8: Finding Your Voice

The asanas of this class help us open the fifth chakra, located in the throat. This chakra is responsible for unlocking our Divine life purpose. We will explore Purvottanasana (intense backward neck stretch), and Dwi Pada Pitham (baby backbend). As you practice these poses, notice how the neck is carefully stretched in both directions, providing awareness of this area, and working on opening it.

In this class, we will also explore a Pratyahara (sense withdrawal) exercise, which helps us focus inward. We will listen carefully for messages from the Divine to help discern our life purpose.

As we approach the culmination of the course, this set of extraordinary asanas will have a powerful effect when it comes to bringing clarity, owning your power, and having a definite sense of purpose.

Purvotanasana

Dvi Pada Pitham

Pratyahara

Reflections and Insights

Body sensations I noticed:

Changes in my breathing:

Emotional release:

Insights from my wisdom body:

Spiritual connection:

Class 9: Meditation

Through this practice you will enter a deep meditative state and invite enlightenment, by way of Divine intervention and timing.

Paschimottanasana

The asana part of this class is less strenuous as we will feel the body in a different, more meditative way. We will do one of the most powerful asanas ever created, Paschimottanasana, the seated forward bend. We will hold this pose for a few minutes to unlock its power. After that, we will do a breathing exercise, and practice sense withdrawal and concentration. A more advanced aspect of yoga, that of deep meditation, happens automatically when the conditions are right. I wish for you the gift of meditation in which you can momentarily calm the mind and fall into the stillness of the moment.

Seated Meditation Pose

How to Have a Yoga Body

Reflections and Insights

Body sensations I noticed:

Changes in my breathing:

Emotional release:

Insights from my wisdom body:

Spiritual connection:

Class 10: Integration Practice

This is the class in which all the benefits of your work come together. Remember to add this practice as a top line to your life, meaning a new positive habit to take care of your body, mind, emotions, and spirit.

You did it! Congratulations!

Reflections and Insights

Body sensations I noticed:

Changes in my breathing:

Emotional release:

Insights from my wisdom body:

Spiritual connection:

FINAL WORDS

Congratulations on the work you have done. By applying the principles of yoga and practicing along with the videos, you have taken a big step toward developing a healthy, vibrant, and shining yoga body. As a way of judging your progress, look back at your journal entries since you started the book, and note how you have changed.

You can also judge your progress by how you feel and how your life is going. If you feel life is getting better, then the practices are bearing fruit. Yoga should bring not only good health but also abundance and pleasure. Owning your light should bring a calm and centered happiness that comes from contentment, self-esteem, and having a life purpose.

Keep in mind that having a yoga body is an ongoing process. The physical practice along with the knowledge you gain are meant to be a way of living. As you continue your journey, and the deeper you go, the more interesting life will get.

MY WISH FOR YOU

I wish you good health.

I wish you clarity in your life purpose.

I wish you the right attitude to continue practicing in a steady way, with no judgement but with discipline.

I wish you abundance and wealth.

I wish you love and compassion.

I wish you an enormous supply of self-esteem.

I wish you a fulfilling and intimate special relationship.

I wish you a loving and supportive community.

I wish you liberation and freedom from the tyranny of negative thinking.

I wish you peace.

I wish you a vibrant yoga body.

ACKNOWLEDGMENTS

Yoga provides a wonderful way to keep us centered, happy, and sane. But no yogi can sustain themselves without a community of supportive people. I am no exception.

My partner, Frank, is the main editor and soul-keeper of the book. Nathalie Jaspar inspired some of the personal stories that I included. She knew they would enhance my message and encouraged me to share them. Nathalie is also the artist behind the beautiful and only drawing in the book, depicting a woman peeling away layers, searching for the Divine. Gloria Dostal took all the beautiful asana photographs.

A group of powerful women help me with business decisions and provide a spiritual container for me to thrive. Among them are Cara, Jayne, and Beth.

Thank you, this book wouldn't exist without you.

My family is a pillar of serenity and support: Mariano, Ana, Viki, Olivia, gracias.

And then there is you, communicating with me over distance and time. I am eternally grateful that you are reading, following the classes, and extending your comments, reviews, and suggestions.

Claudia.

Buenos Aires
February 2022

RESOURCES

Yoga Mat:
I suggest one of these quality mats that provide both comfort and support:
- Jade Yoga Mat
- Jade Travel Yoga Mat
- Manduka Yoga Mat

Yoga Blocks:
- Volcano Cork Yoga Blocks (set of two)

Yoga Blanket:
- Canyon Creek Mexican Yoga Blanket

Neti Pot:
- Natural and Co. Ceramic Neti Pot

Dry Brush:
- ZenMe Dry Brushing Body Brush

Tongue Scraper:
- Pure Earth Essentials Copper Tongue Scraper

Enema Kit:
- Cor-Vital Disposable Enema Bag Kit

Books:

- Hatha Yoga Pradipika, by Swami Muktibodhananda
- The Yoga Sutras of Patanjali, by Swami Satchidananda
- Kundalini: Yoga for The West, by Swami Sivananda Radha

Richard Freeman

- The Art of Vinyasa: Awakening Body and Mind Through the Practice of Ashtanga Yoga
- When Love Comes to Light: Bringing Wisdom from the Bhagavad Gita to Modern Life
- The Mirror of Yoga: Awakening the Intelligence of Body and Mind

Gregor Maehle

- Ashtanga Yoga: Practice and Philosophy
- Pranayama The Breath of Yoga
- Yoga Meditation: Through Mantra, Chakras and Kundalini to Spiritual Freedom
- How To Find Your Life's Divine Purpose: Brain Software for a New Civilization
- Samadhi The Great Freedom

Marianne Williamson

- A Return to Love: Reflections on the Principles of "A Course in Miracles"

- A Woman's Worth
- Illuminata: A Return to Prayer
- The Law of Divine Compensation: On Work, Money, and Miracles

Eckhart Tolle
Audiobooks:
- For Those Who Serve: Practical Guidance for Being of Benefit to Others
- Breaking the Habit of Negative Thinking and Self-Talk
- Sustaining Presence in the Face of Catastrophe: Teachings on Awakening to Our Essential Nature
- Freedom from the World
- The Journey into Yourself
- Touching the Eternal
- Enlightened Relationships

Books:
- A New Earth: Awakening to Your Life's Purpose
- The Power of Now: A Guide to Spiritual Enlightenment
- Practicing the Power of Now: Teachings, Meditations, and Exercises from the Power of Now
- Stillness Speaks

About
THE AUTHOR

Claudia Azula is a yoga teacher and best-selling author.

Her YouTube channel has over 55,000 subscribers and offers weekly yoga classes as well as demonstrations of her private practice.

Subscribe to her newsletter for monthly updates and exclusive personal stories by visiting her website, **ClaudiaYoga.com**

You can also connect with her via these platforms:

- Claudia Azula
- ClaudiaMarinaAzula
- ClaudiaYoga

If you enjoyed this book, Claudia would love to have you post an honest review on Amazon.

Other Books by
THE AUTHOR

Become an Idea Machine

21 Things to Know Before Starting an Ashtanga Yoga Practice

The Power of No